HIDDEN HISTORY
of
DILLON COUNTY

HIDDEN HISTORY
of
DILLON COUNTY

CARLEY WIGGINS

Published by The History Press
Charleston, SC 29403
www.historypress.net

Copyright © 2011 by Carley Wiggins
All rights reserved

First published 2011

Manufactured in the United States

ISBN 978.1.60949.158.1

Library of Congress Cataloging-in-Publication Data

Wiggins, Carley.
Hidden history of Dillon County / Carley Wiggins.
p. cm.
ISBN 978-1-60949-158-1
1. Dillon County (S.C.)--History--Anecdotes. 2. Dillon County (S.C.)--Social life and customs--Anecdotes. 3. Dillon County (S.C.)--Biography--Anecdotes. 4. Country life--South Carolina--Dillon County--History--Anecdotes. I. Title.
F277.D5W535 2011
975.7'85--dc22
2011002396

Notice: The information in this book is true and complete to the best of our knowledge. It is offered without guarantee on the part of the author or The History Press. The author and The History Press disclaim all liability in connection with the use of this book.

All rights reserved. No part of this book may be reproduced or transmitted in any form whatsoever without prior written permission from the publisher except in the case of brief quotations embodied in critical articles and reviews.

This book is dedicated to all the readers who follow and read my weekly articles that are published in the Dillon Herald *newspaper. Without your interest in the articles I write, I would have quit long ago. Hardly a week goes by that I don't receive an e-mail, card or letter or someone just walks up to say that they appreciate what I am doing. Words cannot describe what the hundreds of contacts that I have made with you and your loyalty have meant to me over the past seven years. I must also share this dedication with my wife, Helen, who keeps me going each week with all her help and encouragement. It is with a humble heart that I dedicate to you*

Hidden History of Dillon County

Contents

Acknowledgements	9
Remembering Border Belt Baseball	11
Life on a Tobacco Farm	41
Hog-Killing Time	59
Here Comes the Goat Man!	65
The Maple Swamp Gang	77
The Life and Times of David D. Bethea	91
The Mill Village	101
About the Author	125

Acknowledgements

I would like to thank the following people for their invaluable help with the contents of this book:

"Remembering Border Belt Baseball": Stacey Griffin, Leo (Gabby) Norris, Kromer Stephens and Lloyd Meekins

"Life on a Tobacco Farm": a Dillon farmer

"Hog-Killing Time": Lucille Berry Easterling

"Here Comes the Goat Man!": Don McDowell

"The Maple Swamp Gang": Mary Carmichael Stephens

"The Life and Times of David D. Bethea": Anthony B. Cochran, Dorothy Alford Bethea and Mamie Brown Manning

"The Mill Village": Lonnie Turner, Van Benson and Dalton Sheppard Jr.

Remembering Border Belt Baseball

In 2006, I wrote a three-week series on a semipro football team that Dillon had back in the early sixties called the Dillon Redskins. Since that time, I have had numerous people ask me to do something on the old Border Belt baseball league. I have been a little reluctant to tackle this subject since I was just a small boy when Border Belt baseball got started.

Well, over the past several months I have become more determined to bring back the memories that this once very popular baseball league brought to a lot of people. So many people whom I will mention in this article are deceased, but they could have been your grandfather, father or maybe just a relative or perhaps just someone you saw play. I hope as we talk about these folks in this story, it may bring back some fond memories for you.

I would like to add that if there were not a few men left around who played in this league and some who were affiliated in other ways, if nothing more than as a fan, the telling of this story would not have been possible. As time goes by, I will mention by name each person who helped to bring this story to life.

I want to take you back to the year 1947. The big war had been over for two years. It was a peaceful time around Dillon; the day of the baby boomers had begun, we got electricity for the first time on the farm and I turned seven years old that year and started the second grade at Latta Elementary School. Another significant thing happened in Dillon: the Border Belt baseball league began.

Dillon's Border Belt baseball team during the early years. *First row, left to right*: L.E. "Gabby" Norris, Dudley Saleeby, Bill Scott (umpire), Tom Fletcher, Mendel Rast, Luther Herring, Ike Dunlap. *Second row*: Joel Butler, Joe Morris, Joe Summerlin, Harold Quick, Harvey Blue Bethea, Royce Cottingham, unknown, James Moody. *Top row*: A.D. Pittman. *Courtesy of the children of Royce Cottingham.*

Border Belt baseball lasted for some twenty years in Dillon County, and I will attempt to take you through these years and mention as many players, coaches, batboys and umpires as I can.

As we look back to 1947, radio was very popular, and Dillon had two movie houses that drew a lot of people. George Spradley had a poolroom where the boys would go and shoot pool. The drugstores had soda fountains where the boys and girls would meet and pass away the time. So what did folks do back then for entertainment? They went to baseball games. Every little town and community had a baseball team, and everybody went to the ballgames. This was before the Friday night football games became so popular, and basketball had not caught on. We didn't know what golf was, and the Darlington Raceway had not been built.

Baseball was king. There were some fellows who were much better players than others, and through this story I will highlight some who were very talented. In 1947, Jackie Robinson became the first African American player to make it to the Major Leagues with the Brooklyn

Remembering Border Belt Baseball

Dodgers. The best natural hitter to ever play the game, Ted Williams of the Boston Red Sox, was driving the American League pitchers crazy trying to keep the ball away from the best eye in baseball.

As I understand it, the Border Belt League came off what was called the Pee Dee League. When the name changed to Border Belt, Dr. Lawrence McIntyre, who ran a drugstore, and Mr. Fred Quick, who owned a barbershop were the directors of the Dillon team.

Dillon didn't even have a field with lights; there was a field at East Elementary School where the high school games were played. Latta had lights in 1947, and the athletic field was right beside Highway 301, where the middle school is located today. The Dillon and Latta teams worked out their schedule so that both teams could play their home games in Latta.

The photo that accompanies this article, courtesy of the Royce Cottingham children, is the earliest photo of the Dillon Border Belt team that I have been able to find. Only two of these men are surviving: L.E. "Gabby" Norris and A.D. Pittman. Ike Dunlap passed away in 2009 at the age of eighty-nine.

Dudley Saleeby was the coach of the 1947 team, and he coached a lot of baseball in his life, including so many years of Little League ball, which helped a lot of youngsters while they were growing up. I guess the man who finally convinced me to write this story was Gabby Norris. His wife, Mary, wrote me a letter saying how much she liked to read my articles. A few weeks back she called me, and while we were talking, I asked if I could speak to her husband. When I hung up the phone, I knew this story had to be written. The next week we went up to Wallace, South Carolina, where the Norrises now live, to visit, and as I listened to him talk about old-time baseball, his eyes lit up like a kid who was going to start his first Little League game.

It didn't take me long to find out that this man had a genuine love for the sport of baseball. Gabby is now eighty-seven, but his health is beginning to fail. Gabby was the catcher for the Dillon team, and I had the opportunity to see Gabby play several times after Dillon built its own stadium where it still sits on West Main Street Extension.

Gabby Norris may have been one of the best defensive catchers to ever come out of this part of the country. I remember seeing him streak down

Royce Cottingham on the mound for the New Bern Bears. *Courtesy of the children of Royce Cottingham.*

the first base line to back up the first baseman on an infield ground ball. Sometimes he would literally beat the runner to first base.

If a ball was popped up behind the plate or along the sidelines, Gabby was going to get that ball most all of the time. He would also guard the plate as good as anyone. Gabby didn't mind making contact to keep a score from coming in. Gabby was not a great hitter but was known to come through in the clutch. What he lacked in offense, he more than made up in defense. Also, he could really intimidate a batter with his constant chatter.

Gabby Norris played baseball a long time and would play anywhere somebody wanted to get up a game. He played ball in the military during World War II and caught some Major League pitchers. Gabby's playing days were ended in 1956 when he suffered a heart attack.

Remembering Border Belt Baseball

Gabby moved to Wallace over forty years ago and went into the drapery business. At one time, he employed over one hundred people. The Dillon Stadium was completed in 1948, and both the high school and Border Belt teams used the same baseball field.

The teams that were in the Border Belt League when it first started were Dillon; Lake View; Latta; Rowland, North Carolina; Fair Bluff, North Carolina; and Whiteville, North Carolina. Over the years, some of these teams dropped out and other towns came into the league.

The parks were filled at each game. I remember going to high school and some Border Belt games back in the late forties and you couldn't get a seat; people would be standing all along the sidelines. The Border Belt players were not paid. They simply played because they loved the game. As we get further into the history of the players, we will see where several of these players could have perhaps played Major League baseball, but there were circumstances that kept them from going to big-time baseball.

I will also tell you as much as I could find out about some of the other teams that played in the league, as well as some people who played for them. I want to start with the Dillon team when it started back in 1947. The Dillon team was first called the Blue Sox. Some of the first players were L.E. "Gabby" Norris, catcher; Jimmy Davis, who was a brother of Thad Davis Sr., M.D. Davis and Christine Skipper all played first base; along with Harvey Blue Bethea, brother of Patsy Bethea Lester and our county treasurer for many years, Mary Louise Parham.

Ike Dunlap played second base. Stacey Griffin, one of the players I will be highlighting in this story, played at shortstop, and Kromer Stephens, another player I will be talking about, played third base. In the outfield were Joe Morris in left field, Harold Quick in center field and A.D. Pittman in right field. Mr. Pittman is now eighty-four and makes his home in Raleigh, North Carolina.

The pitchers were Royce Cottingham (whom I will be telling you more about soon), Luther Herring, Joe Minshew and Tom Fletcher. Other members of the early team were Mendel Rast, James Moody, Joel Butler and Joe Summerlin. Now keep in mind that there were new players coming out all the time, and I will be mentioning all those that I know about as time goes by.

Stacey Griffin, 1947. *Courtesy of Stacey and Sylvia Scott Griffin.*

Kromer Stephens, 1949, University of South Carolina. *Courtesy of Mr. and Mrs. Kromer Stephens.*

Remembering Border Belt Baseball

The player we will be spotlighting first is Royce Cottingham, who is a legend among those who remember seeing him play baseball. I must admit that I don't remember seeing Royce play, but as I listen to folks a little older than I talk about this man, he had to be a remarkable player. Royce Cottingham played three sports in high school and graduated in 1946.

Mr. Austin Smith, an old-time baseball player himself back in the 1930s, was a Major League scout here in Dillon. Mr. Smith took Royce right out of high school to Atlanta for a tryout with the triple A team the Atlanta Crackers. After seeing Royce pitch, the Atlanta manager offered him a job, but Royce declined, saying that he had never been farther from home than Florence and he was young and dating real heavy at the time.

He later would try a stint in semipro ball with the New Bern Bears in the coastal plains class D league. Royce played out the 1947 and 1948 season with the Bears. He was paid fifty dollars and a meal ticket per week. This was a far cry from what ballplayers make today.

While at New Bern, Royce played against local fellows Stacey Griffin and Kromer Stephens, who played some semipro ball. One day while pitching batting practice, Royce was hit in the cheek from a sharp line drive. He stated that he never could get back in shape, and he came back to Dillon to play several years of Border Belt ball.

Royce was a left-hander and was a good control pitcher. His most effective pitch was what was known as a drop in that day; today it would be called a slider. People who saw him pitch said he could make the ball drop two feet just before it reached the batter.

Gabby Norris, who caught a lot of pitchers in his career as well as some big league pitchers, told me that Royce Cottingham was the best pitcher he ever caught. Gabby said that he could lay his mitt on his left leg and when Royce threw the ball, he would not have to move the mitt an inch. It was told to me that Royce once struck out nineteen batters in one game. I have not been able to document this, but I read that it was not unusual for him to strike out twelve to sixteen batters in a single game.

One season in Border Belt ball, he went undefeated for the year. Many folks say that Royce Cottingham could have played Major League ball. He was known by opposing teams as "that left-hander from Dillon." Former state senator Gene Carmichael stated, "I hated to bat against that guy."

Many people say that Royce Cottingham was the best left-hander to come from Dillon. Some of the younger folks say that Larry Herring, who almost made it to the big show before suffering an injury, was the best. Then there was a little guy from Latta called "Snout" Hyatt who was an awesome left-handed pitcher. But Royce Cottingham would have ranked among the best.

Royce Cottingham spent many years in the department store business selling men's clothing and shoes, as well as serving on the Dillon police force. He was a good-natured fellow, very easy to talk to. Royce passed away on December 7, 2005, at the age of seventy-eight. He is greatly missed by family and friends. He also left a great legacy for those who watched him play the sport of baseball.

As we move a little forward in time, the league started in 1947, and Dillon won the league championship that year. As I was told, John David Hilton got a whopping $100 for hitting the first home run in the new stadium. John David had a brother Bill who also played. The Hilton brothers were sons of Mr. John Hilton, who was a building contractor in Dillon. Mr. Hilton was an avid baseball fan and sometimes would wind up in some arguments that would arise on the field. Ken McCutcheon, who was at one time a coach for Dillon High School and was in the hardware business, as well as a Dillon magistrate, played Border Belt ball and was a good player in the outfield for Dillon.

Lawrence Rogers, older brother of Johnny Rogers, played for Dillon and was rated as a first-class player. Lawrence played a lot of baseball, including American Legion for several teams, and went on to receive a scholarship to Wofford College. Other players who were mentioned were Gene Evans and Gerald Moody, who went on to coach at Berkley High School. Hubert Morris and Red Bethea also played.

Some of these fellows may have only played one year, but many played several years. Bentley Hardaway, the undisputed mayor of Bunker Hill, caught some for the Dillon team. Doug Rogers, who was father of school Superintendant Ray Rogers, played Border Belt ball. In reading some old newspaper clippings from that time, Dillon had some good teams, as did Latta and Lake View, which I will be telling you more about in time to come.

Remembering Border Belt Baseball

Mr. A.D. Pittman, who is eighty-four and lives in Raleigh, told me about the time he got a home run off a strikeout. He said he took a third strike and the catcher dropped the ball. He took off for first base, and the catcher threw the ball over the first baseman's head into right field, so Pittman rounded first and headed for second. Well, the right fielder made a wild throw, and to make a long story short, he wound up with a home run that started off as a strikeout.

Before we get to our next spotlight player, I want to tell you about another whom several men have commented about as being one of the best baseball players to come from Dillon. Babe King worked for Dillon Service Company for years and was also quite a baseball player. It was told to me that he was not only a great first baseman but an excellent hitter as well. He made few mistakes and helped Dillon to win a lot of ballgames. As I understand, Babe went on to play in an industrial league in the upper part of the state.

Our next spotlight player is Stacey Griffin. Stacey was perhaps one of the best all-around athletes to come out of Dillon High School. He excelled in both football and baseball. He was an outstanding baseball player, and his most valuable asset was consistency. Stacey didn't have many bad games. He had the ability to play most anywhere on the field, but he usually played at shortstop.

In high school, he never batted below .500, and his first year in Border Belt ball, he led the league with a blistering .511 batting average. Stacey had the ideal size for a baseball player at six feet, two inches and 180 pounds. He had good speed and could hit the long ball as well as base hits. Pitchers didn't like to pitch against Stacey because he was a tough out. Stacey attracted the attention of a lot of scouts who wanted him on their teams.

He told me that perhaps his biggest mistake was turning down a full scholarship to North Carolina State to play baseball. I agreed with him that athletes should go ahead and get their education because that is something you can never take away from them. But in this day and time, the bonuses that some of these athletes get are almost impossible to turn down.

Stacey signed with the Detroit Tigers for $1,000; I guess that sounded like a lot of money back then. In 1948, Stacey reported for spring training with the Tigers' AAA farm club in Thomasville, Georgia. He played with Thomasville for three months and was shipped to another AAA club in Williamsport, Pennsylvania, where he continued to be an outstanding shortstop and hitter, usually batting third or fourth in the lineup. After a short stay at Williamsport, he was again moved to the AAA team in Smithfield Selma, North Carolina, where he continued to play good ball.

He drove in several game-winning runs for the Tobacco League team, and it looked like Stacey was headed for Major League baseball when an old football injury to his shoulder began to plague him. Playing every day did not give the injury time to heal. In the spring of 1949, Stacey reported back to the team, but after a while the pain in his shoulder returned. As time went by, the pain became so intense that he began to think of giving up his lifetime dream of playing in the Major Leagues.

Stacey was making $350 month paying AAA ball, which was pretty good money in 1949, but he realized that he couldn't play every day with the pain in his shoulder. I guess if they had the medical technology back then, perhaps he could have overcome the injury and gone on to the big time. Instead, Stacey Griffin returned to Dillon, and played Border Belt baseball in 1950 and 1951. Playing a couple of games a week was not like trying to play every day. Stacey still says he regrets not taking that scholarship that he was offered, but it seems that he didn't do too badly in life.

He retired in 1990 with forty years of service with Carolina Power and Light. He joined the National Guard as an enlisted man and went all the way to brigadier general with thirty-one years of service to his state and country. Stacey and his wife, Sylvia Scott Griffin, seem to live a comfortable life, but has Stacey Griffin forgotten about baseball? Not in this writer's mind; just talk to him and watch the glint in his eye when he tells you about his baseball days. I think every young man who has ever played baseball dreams of walking on to a big league field wearing that uniform. I don't believe Stacey Griffin ever lost that dream.

Now we will look back a little further in time to the late 1940s and up to about 1953. We will talk about some of the players who came along in this time frame. Some played only maybe one year, while others may have played for several years. We will wind up the early Dillon Border belt team. Before we finish the story, we will come back to Dillon for a look at some of the later teams.

Remembering Border Belt Baseball

In the early fifties, Border Belt ball was going strong. The parks would be filled every night with the fans looking for another exciting night of baseball. There were many dedicated fans who would go to each game to support their teams. Since starting this story, I have heard many stories about players and certain games.

There were some die-hard fans back then. I was told a story about some Pittman fellows who would go to each game, and one night a terrible storm began to brew about game time. The rain began to come down in buckets, but these fellows still sat there and told the players "come on guys, its not going to rain, we want to see a ballgame."

It was said that Dr. Vic Branford, who was a surgeon in Dillon at that time, would go to almost every game. One night, Stacey Griffin got a pretty nasty cut from a player's cleat, and Dr. Branford came over to take a look at Stacey's leg. He told Stacey, "You better come on down to my office with me and let's get that leg stitched up." Stacey said the doctor didn't charge him a dime because he loved the ballgames that much.

Fair Bluff, North Carolina, had a team at that time, and it was noted for playing pretty rough. One night while playing Dillon, a fight broke out on the field, and before long all the stands were emptied on both sides and everybody got into the fight. It was said that Mr. John Hilton jumped right into the middle of the crowd. I don't know if the game continued or not after the fight was finally broken up.

Cole Jacobs was a left-handed pitcher for Fair Bluff. It was said that he had a great fastball and a wicked curve that was very hard to hit. June Waddell caught for Fair Bluff, and some say he may have been the best all-around catcher in Border Belt ball. He had a good arm, and few people stole bases on him. He was also rated as a great hitter.

Rowland, North Carolina, had an early team and I don't know a lot about the team except that it had a pitcher named Nate Andrews who had played Major League ball for the old Boston Braves. An old newspaper clipping that I found said that Andrews was usually used in relief. If the Rowland team had the lead in the first half of the game, they would bring in Andrews, and the game was usually over. For about four innings, Andrews was almost impossible to hit. Rowland had another pitcher named Ralph Brake who was an outstanding pitcher. Bill Britt also pitched for Rowland.

Getting back to the Dillon team, during this time, Van Benson was the batboy, and he has been an invaluable help in the telling of this story because he has an excellent memory. Umpires kind of came and went; most anybody whom they could pick up with any baseball knowledge usually served as an umpire. Mr. Bill Scott called balls and strikes at a lot of games, and Harold Cadell, who also played for a Mill Village team, umpired the bases.

Clarence Stewart, who now lives in Effingham, played some good ball for Dillon. Clarence played in center field and hit .348 one season. Jack Carter, former police chief of Dillon who is now deceased, was a good pitcher for the Dillon team. Tommy Morris was a slick fielding shortstop and a good hitter for Dillon for a couple of years in the early fifties. Julian Moody played second base for the team.

Some other men who have been mentioned to me who played for Dillon in the early days were Bob Stutts, Jack Skipper and Roy Watts, who did some catching. Everett Moody played some but went on to be a better golfer than a baseball player. Milton Morris, who was a Latta guy and I think played some Border Belt ball with that town, also played some with Dillon. I remember he was a very good player.

Bill Douglas, who lives right across from the park, played with Dillon. Bill Pittman also played, as did Bill Nettles, who worked for the phone company, and David Tyndall, who had a younger brother who became quite a ballplayer. Craig Stephens—retired postal carrier—and Doug Stanton—who worked for Winn-Dixie for years and has been the meat manager for Carl's Food Center for a good while—played the outfield and did some catching for Dillon. Doug has also been a great help on this story.

The next player we will be spotlighting is Kromer Stephens. Kromer played Border Belt ball for about six years. Kromer played high school ball at Dillon High School and joined the navy right out of high school. When he came back from serving his country, he started playing with the Dillon Border Belt team, usually at third base. He was also known to play at other infield positions.

In the fall of 1947, Kromer enrolled at the University of South Carolina. He went out for the baseball team in the spring of 1948 and had a good showing in spring practice, but he was cut because the team was loaded down with more experienced players. He played for the

Three of the best in their older days: Stacey Griffin, Royce Cottingham and Kromer Stephens. *Courtesy of Mr. and Mrs. Kromer Stephens.*

Brooklyn-Cayce All-Stars that year and led the team in hitting with a .380 batting average.

In 1949, he again went out for baseball at USC. The regular second baseman had signed a pro baseball contract, and Kromer Stephens wound up with the starting second base position. The Gamecocks played a 21-game schedule that year with a 15-6 win-loss record, and Kromer batted in the clean-up spot and hit .325 that year. The Gamecocks finished in second place in the Southern Conference, and Kromer was named to the all-southern conference second team.

Kromer returned to USC in the fall of 1949, but the funds he had received under the GI Bill were running out. Unable to get any further financial aid, Kromer came back to Dillon in January 1950. He signed a baseball contract with the Boston Braves in the spring of 1950 and went to Pensacola, Florida, for a few weeks before he was optioned to the Wilson, North Carolina team.

After a short while, he asked to be relieved of his contract and came back to Dillon, even though he was playing good ball. He got tired of the daily grind of the long bus trips and decided to give up his dream of making the big time. There was not much future in baseball back then unless you were in the Major Leagues. I remember when Ted Williams became the first player to make $125,000 per year. That seemed like an awful lot of money, and it was good money back then, but most players played for the league minimum. Many players make that much a week now.

Kromer was always known as a steady ballplayer who made few errors and was quick on his feet, a good glove man and a steady hitter. Kromer Stephens, like some of the other players I have mentioned, could have made it to big-time baseball with the right breaks. In talking to Kromer face to face, it was very evident that he loved the game of baseball. Kromer is retired with thirty-one years with the U.S. post office and also served two terms as a Dillon County councilman.

Now we will talk about the Border Belt team from Lake View, a small town that has always been rich in sports history. It is amazing to walk into Lake View High School and see all the trophies that this school has won in the school's history. Lake View is a town that backs its sports program to the fullest, regardless of what sport it might be.

Lake View Border Belt team, early fifties. *Top row, left to right*: Amos Brewer (manager), Lide Miller, Gene Carmichael, Rhett Gleason, J.D. Rodgers, Dean Bryant, Jerry Page, Dewey Proctor, Robert Garris. *Middle row*: Phil Herring, unknown, Bobby Perritt, Jimmy King, unknown, Billy Page, Wilton Page, Marvin Suggs. *Front row, third from left*: Johnny Gaddy, rest unknown. *Courtesy of Lide Miller.*

Remembering Border Belt Baseball

Lake View had a Border Belt baseball team for several years, and like all Lake View teams, it played hard and played to win. The best I can gather, the Lake View team was called the Rockets in the early years, and they won the league championship in 1949, playing against some pretty good ball teams.

The 1949 team was loaded with talent, including four brothers. Mr. Jesse Ford was the manager of the '49 team and was also a good baseball player in his day. Mr. Ford was active in a lot of things, having served as mayor of Lake View and also in the state legislature.

Gene Carmichael, former state senator, played first base and was called "Hollywood"; just why I don't know. He was long and lanky and was known as a good fielder. Mr. Carmichael is one of the few surviving members from that team. Kromer Stephens, who played one year at Lake View, was on the '49 team at second base. Glenn McDaniel played some for the Mullins team but played at Lake View in 1949. He was a slick fielding shortstop and a very good hitter.

Reuben Rogers, one of the four Rogers brothers who played on the team, played at third base. He is still living today and works part time. Robert Rogers, another brother, played left field, and Dick Rogers played center field. Dick was rated as a good player who played a good outfield and was a good left-handed hitter. He could hit the long ball with power.

I am not quite sure who the starting right fielder was, but the team had several players who could play most anywhere. The catcher was the fourth Rogers brother, the late Jasper D. "Pete" Rogers, a former sheriff and probate judge in Dillon County for much of his life. The pitcher was Schubert Hayes, who was said to have very good control and threw a variety of curve balls and could hit the strike zone almost anywhere he wanted.

Lynwood "Slim" McCormick was from Marietta, North Carolina. He was tall and didn't appear to have much on the ball, but his style seemed to intimidate opposing batters, and he got the job done. Another pitcher was Bennie "Mose" Hendricks, who was recruited from Conway. It was said that Hendricks threw the fastest pitches ever thrown in the Lake View Park. There were no timers back then, but some thought he threw the ball at one hundred miles per hour.

Other players who were on the 1949 Lake View team were Norris Baker, Roland Spivey, Robert Smith and Osh Elvington, who was later a manager for the team, along with Amos Brewer. Maxie Miller played on that team, along with G.C. Baker.

I don't know exactly when the Lake View team folded, but I do know it lasted through 1953. A lot of the Lake View players originated from a team that played at Fork.

Carlton Sawyer from Mullins called me to say that when the Mullins team folded, a lot of players, including himself, came to Lake View to play. He mentioned Herbert Dozier, Jerry Rogers, Herbert Fowler, R.M. Fowler, Zack Sawyer, Heywood Cook and Robert Cook.

Dewey Proctor, who was an athletic legend around Lake View, also played for the team. He played high school sports, college ball and professional football. Dewey also played some Border Belt ball; he played at first base and was a great power hitter. It was said that he hit perhaps the longest home run at Lake View. For a big man, he was very fast on his feet.

Bobby Perritt, former owner of the Lake View IGA, played along with Wade Miller, Paul Sanderson, Jerry Page, Robert Garris, Dean Bryant, Rhett Gleason, Phil Herring, Jimmy King, Marvin Suggs, Hal Cook, Wilton Page and the late Billy G. Page, whose research has been a valuable help in writing this story.

This one is for you Mary: C.W. Rogers played some good ball for the Lake View team. He was a steady and consistent fielder, a good hit and run man and could hit the ball most anywhere he wanted. The last Lake View player I will talk about, and my spotlight player, is Lide Miller. I had a chance to sit down with Mr. Miller and his wife, Hazel, and I don't remember when I have had a more enjoyable visit. Lide Miller was born December 2, 1918, which would make him the oldest surviving Border Belt player I have found.

As I sat and listened to this grand old gentleman talk about his baseball days, it was just like being there watching him. I don't think I have ever talked to a man who loved the sport more than him. Lide Miller starting playing baseball as a teenager and played until 1953. He played for over twenty years, starting with country teams. He played with teams at Barnesville, North Carolina, and Marietta, North Carolina, as well as Lake View or anywhere else that needed him.

He just loved to play. Mr. Miller said he played about every position but did a lot of pitching. He could throw a good curve as well as a good

Remembering Border Belt Baseball

Lide Miller, a great lover of baseball. *Photo by Helen Lane Wiggins.*

fastball. He showed me how he would grip the ball to throw a curve. I believe the man would play today if his health would permit.

Lide Miller played one of his last games in Mullins on August 26, 1953, while his wife watched from their car. Later that night, their daughter was born. That is what you call loving the game. Lide Miller never dreamed of playing pro ball; he just loved to play.

We will look at the Latta team now, and even though I haven't been able to get as much information on the Latta team as I would like to have had, I will tell you what I know.

From the 1940s and for many years to follow, the Latta stadium was located where the middle school is now located on Highway 301. Home plate would have been just a few yards from where the first stoplight coming south from Dillon is located. All the schools that were in that area, including the high school and two elementary schools, have burned since that time and have been replaced with the present buildings. Latta was a real baseball town back in that time, having already produced two Major League players: Mr. Norman "Bub" McMillan and Mr. Frank Ellerbe Sr. Mr. McMillan played for the New York Yankees in the 1920s and played in the 1922 World Series. Mr. Ellerbe started his Major League career with the Washington Senators in 1919; later he was traded to the St. Louis Browns, who came close to winning the American League pennant in 1922.

Back in the late forties and early fifties, Latta High School won four class B baseball state championships, going undefeated for four years, and another year, the same basic team won seventeen games in a row before losing in the lower state finals. Later in 1966, Latta again won the state championship.

When Latta got started in the Border Belt League, the town had some already seasoned players to choose from. Jerry Johnson, older brother of Alex "Buddy" Johnson, played first base and also did some pitching. Earl Atkinson Jr. was a left-handed second baseman who played some good baseball. Frank Ellerbe Jr. played shortstop for Latta and also played for the University of South Carolina.

Milton Morris, who also played some for Dillon, played at third base for Latta and was a multitalented ballplayer. Chester Taylor, a former county councilman from Dillon County, played center field. S.J. Allen, who was in the tire business for years, played in the outfield, along with John Coleman, who played on the Border Belt All-Star team in 1947.

Howard Webster, a big guy from Floyd Dale, played right field and could hit the ball with good power. Red Lane was one of the first catchers for Latta, and it was said he was a good one. Some of the first pitchers for Latta were Charlie Long and Coy Jackson. I never saw either of these fellows pitch, but several people have said that Long was a small man but a very good pitcher. I understand he is still living in the Chicago area. Coy Jackson was the Gulf Oil distributor in Dillon for many years. Both Long and Jackson were named to the 1947 All-Star team.

Remembering Border Belt Baseball

Latta wound up in third place in the league in its first year with a 12-6 record. Players came and went after the first year, and again I don't know when the Latta team dropped out of Border Belt, but I believe it lasted through about 1953 or 1954.

Alex "Buddy" Johnson played various positions, including shortstop, second base and center field. Buddy went on to be a coach at Latta and still lives in Latta today. Jimmy Johnson, a younger brother of Buddy, played some for Latta. He is now a retired minister. Harold Benton came on to do some catching, a position he had played in high school. Leon Maxwell, who came to Latta and coached for several years, played some great second base for the Border Belt team. Bill Nettles, who played some for Dillon, also played at Latta. R.J. Lane, a brother of Red Lane, pitched some for Latta. Malcolm "Mutt" Miles, a tall lanky fellow, pitched for the team.

The name Cecil Snipes was also mentioned. Carl Hyatt, who was just a teenager in high school at the time and a man who played a lot of Border Belt ball in the sixties, said he played about eight games for the Latta team when Frank Ellerbe was out.

Now the last player we will talk about and our spotlight player is the legend, J.W. "Snout" Hyatt. I wrote an article about Snout Hyatt in July 2004, and I mentioned him being the best small baseball player I ever saw play the game, but I may have been mistaken: he could have been the best period. Snout Hyatt played one sport and that was baseball, and he played as hard as anyone ever played the game.

Snout came to Latta High School in the eighth grade from Floyd Dale, where he was already an accomplished baseball player. I think sometimes the reason he played so hard was because of his size. He knew he had to excel because he was playing with guys so much larger than he was. Snout Hyatt played five years of varsity baseball, which is almost unheard of.

He changed the way people felt about baseball in the whole county and surrounding areas. People came from miles away to see the master pitch. Snout wasn't hard to spot on the field; he was always the smallest man on the field and the one with the largest nose, from which he received his nickname. Players from opposing teams would take one look at him and remark that this couldn't be the pitcher they had heard so much about, but all it took was one trip to the plate to change their minds.

Latta players Harold Benton, J.W. "Snout" Hyatt and Mutt Miles. *Author's collection.*

Stacey Griffin, who was a better than average baseball player and hit over .500 in Border Belt ball, shared a story with me. He said the first time he batted against Snout, on the first pitch, Snout threw him one of his devastating fastballs. Vondell Lee, who was the umpire, called it a strike. Stacey said he stepped out of the batter's box and said, "Vondell, how can you call that a strike?" Mr. Lee replied, "Because that is what it was." Stacey shot back, "I didn't even see the pitch and I don't believe you did either." I don't know how many baseball records Snout Hyatt holds, but I am sure they will never be broken at Latta High School. In the five years that he played, the team won four state championships and went undefeated for the four years. During the fifth year, the team won seventeen games before losing in the lower state finals.

Remembering Border Belt Baseball

Even though Snout Hyatt has been deceased for forty-one years, having lost his life in an automobile accident at the age of twenty-four on the way home from a baseball game, he still remains the most talked about baseball player among people old enough to remember him. During one of the last high school baseball games that I went to, which was a good many years ago, the pitcher was getting belted by everyone who came to bat. A man who was leaning against the fence and appeared to have had a few drinks shouted, "If that was Snout Hyatt out there, they wouldn't be hitting that ball like that." A lot of the young people in the crowd had no idea who he was talking about, but as I sat there and let my mind float back in time, I said to myself, "Mister, you are so right."

We have covered a lot of baseball, and now we start a new era in the Border Belt baseball league. We have talked about a lot of players who played for a period from 1947 to the mid-1950s. I don't know exactly the year that Dillon, Lake View and Latta dropped out of Border Belt ball, but the best I can determine was somewhere around 1955. Dillon may have played another year or two longer than that.

The Border Belt League continued with mostly North Carolina teams. In the year 1961, Lloyd Meekins had a Sunday afternoon country baseball team where the fellows would get together for a good afternoon of baseball. During that time, a lot of the players expressed a desire to try and get back into the Border Belt League. At this time, the league consisted mostly of teams from across the border in North Carolina.

Lloyd got in touch with Mr. Levy Bridgers from Bladenboro, who was president of the league at that time, and Mr. Bridgers told Lloyd that the league had a full roster of teams at that time, consisting of six teams. In June 1961, Mr. Bridgers called to say that the Fayetteville, North Carolina team had dropped out and the Dillon team could join if they wanted to.

So the Dillon team was back in the Border Belt League and became known as the Dillon Red Legs, a team that would last until 1965. The league consisted in 1961 of teams in Dillon, Pembroke, Rowland, Lumberton, Bladenboro and Whiteville. The Dillon team came into the league with a good roster of ballplayers, and I will try to the best of my ability to name each one before we finish this story.

Lloyd Meekins was the owner and manager of the team and was assisted by Coaches A.Z. Britt Sr. and Herbert "Monk" Meekins. The year 1961 was a learning year for the Red Legs, but they held their own with such teams as Bladenboro and Whiteville, who were the powerhouses of the league at that time.

Ansel Tyndall played a lot of baseball for Latta High School and came to the Red Legs as their starting catcher. Tyndall was a good hitter and scored a lot of runs for the team. In 1963, Tyndall went for a tryout with the Baltimore Orioles at their spring training camp, but they chose another catcher over him, so he came back to play for the Red Legs. Johnny Barfield, who played three sports at Latta High School, was the first baseman for the team. Barfield was a pretty good-sized fellow but was fast on his feet for a big man. He could hit the long ball with good power.

Ansel Tyndall at spring camp with the Baltimore Orioles, 1963. *Courtesy of Laurie Arnette.*

Remembering Border Belt Baseball

Johnny Barfield was a key player for the Dillon Red Legs. *Courtesy of Mrs. Johnny Barfield.*

Johnny Barfield played hard at any sport in which he participated and never showed much emotion whether he hit a home run or struck out. Barfield tried out with the Pittsburgh Pirates but could not negotiate a proper bonus so he came back home. Johnny Barfield passed away in 2006.

Lloyd Meekins was real high on second baseman Robert Peele, a guy I didn't know. Meekins said he could always depend on Peele to be at the games and play some good infield for the Red Legs. Robert Peele is also deceased. Bill Watts also played some second base for the team and was rated as a good player. Richard "Monkey" Christmas played shortstop for the Red Legs. He was a slick fielder and a good base hit man. Christmas was also an outstanding ballplayer for Dillon High School in both baseball and football. He has been living in Nebraska for many years.

Jimmy King played third base for the Red Legs. King played a lot of baseball in his life; he was playing with the Lake View Border Belt team back in the early fifties. Lester Webster played left field for the team for a long time. Webster was a good hitter; some newspaper articles mention that he would get as many as four hits in a game. Webster is deceased. Robert Snipes, a man I don't know a lot about, played both infield and outfield for the Red Legs. Bobby Rogers, a man for whom I have a lot of respect, played in the outfield for the Red Legs. Bobby is retired and lives in Dillon.

Red Ransom came from McColl to play right field for the team. Ransom was said to also be a good player. Ransom is deceased, I was told. Cicero McLellan, a left-hander who came from Marion, was an early pitcher for the Red Legs. McLellan could throw a variety of pitches and had pretty good control.

A 1961 newspaper clipping reports that he beat a strong Bladenboro team, allowing only four hits and striking out twelve batters. Carl Hyatt, who played his high school ball at Latta, was also a pitcher for the Red Legs. Hyatt was a right-hander and won some games for the Red Legs in 1961. He was also a good man in relief and could play most any position as well as being a good shortstop. Carl still lives in Latta.

Billy Bullard, who was known as the "Iron Man," pitched for the team and was a Marion native. Bullard was said to have good endurance and could hold his own with most hitters. Gerald Turner also pitched some for the Red Legs in the first year. Lloyd Meekins remembered Gerald as a pretty good right-hander. Gerald is deceased. Gene Lewellen played infield for the team. He was a good base hitter and had a lot of runs batted in. Gene went on to become a Baptist minister but passed away very young.

Ken Jackson was a strong right-handed pitcher for the Red Legs and a very good hitter. Ken played some outstanding baseball for Dillon High School. He lost a bout with cancer a few years back. His brother Lowell Jackson also played some for the Red Legs. Lowell still lives in Dillon. Jimmy Renfrow was an outstanding shortstop for the team; he and his wife raised a fine family. Jimmy still lives in Lake View.

The Red Legs had a good year in their first year in the league, winning more games than they lost, but a powerful Whiteville, North Carolina team behind the pitching of Vic Davis, a former Major Leaguer, and R.C. Kinlaw won the league championship.

Remembering Border Belt Baseball

Six of the Dillon Red Legs most valuable. Left to right: Johnny Barfield, Ansel Tyndall, Carl Hyatt, Robert Peele, Jimmy King, Red Lanier and batboy Mickey Meekins. *Courtesy of Mrs. Johnny Barfield.*

The Red Legs had a pretty good year in 1961, playing against some pretty strong teams that had been together for a good while. When the 1962 season came along, the Red Legs were primed and ready to play for the league championship. The league had pretty much the same teams as it had in 1961. The Red Legs had a lot of the same players back from 1961, and a lot of new players came to play with the Red Legs to give them the added strength to contend for the league title.

One great added asset for the Red Legs would come from Darlington in former Major Leaguer Harry Byrd. Harry Byrd went to the big leagues back when the Philadelphia Athletics were still in the American League. Byrd was a right-handed pitcher and performed well for the Athletics and manager/owner Connie Mack, who was with the Athletics for fifty years.

Byrd was good enough to be named rookie of the year in the American League. Later on, Byrd was traded to the New York Yankees along with Roger Maris, who would break the home run record of Babe Ruth. After playing with the Yankees for a few years, Byrd was traded to the Detroit Tigers, where he would end his career after receiving an injury to his arm.

Byrd came back to Darlington, where he now has a highway named for him. Harry Byrd still loved baseball, so he called Lloyd Meekins about playing for the Red Legs. Meekins, of course, accepted his offer, and Harry Byrd became a pitcher for the Dillon Red Legs.

Another addition to the team's pitching staff was Wyman Taylor, former baseball coach for Dillon High School. Taylor was a left-hander and had a good variety of pitches. Curt Allen came from the Little Rock area and pitched some for the Red Legs. Still another pitcher who played for the Red Legs was Ebie McElveen, who came from Lake City.

Now keep in mind that a lot of the pitchers could play other positions, so on a given night you might see a guy who had pitched on Tuesday playing shortstop on Thursday. Such was the case with McElveen and several other players. Bobby Berry, who played high school ball at Latta, was a left-hander and pitched some for the Red Legs, as well as playing first base and the outfield. Berry was also a good hitter with a real high batting average.

Harold Grice, who served as Dillon County sheriff for over twenty years, was also quite a baseball player. Grice also came out of Floydale, and I believe that for a boy to live in Floydale, he had to play baseball. Floydale was known as the Latta High School farm club, and a lot of good players came from there. Sheriff Grice played for Latta High and also for the Red Legs as a pitcher and first baseman.

Hiram Cook played center field for the Red Legs almost from the beginning of the team. Lloyd Meekins said that Cook was a good base hitter, usually batting in the leadoff position, because he was fast and a good base runner. Jack Lee Morrison was a good all-around athlete, having played three sports at Latta High School. I remember Jack Lee well, as I was a classmate of his. Morrison played for the Red Legs; he could play any position but usually played second base or shortstop. Jack Lee Morrison became a farmer and died a young man in his early fifties.

The Red Legs had some good talent on the 1962 team, and in researching old newspaper articles, it seems that the Red Legs were up there at the top of the Border Belt League most of the 1962 season. Just a few examples of some games that year were the Friday night in June they beat the Pembroke Braves by a score of 3–2. Harry Byrd gave up four hits in seven innings, with Carl Hyatt coming on in the seventh and holding the Braves hitless the rest of the game. Ansel Tyndall, Johnny Barfield, Lester Webster, Jimmy King and Harry Byrd all went two for four in hitting. Red Lanier had a triple for the night.

Remembering Border Belt Baseball

On August 3, 1962, the Red Legs had a 12-7 record, just behind a strong Whiteville team at 13-6. The Red Legs would beat the Whiteville Leafs that night by a score of 8–3. Wyman Taylor was the winning pitcher, striking out twelve batters. Johnny Barfield had a three-run home run for the Red Legs.

Again keep in mind that these fellows did not get paid to play; they played for the love of the game. In talking to Lloyd Meekins, the owner and manager of the team, he said he had a lot of good memories of the team. He said a lot of the guys might not play but just a few games, but there were a few who stuck with him until the team finally folded from a lack of interest. By the year 1962, a lot of homes were beginning to get televisions and Friday night football was gaining more popularity, and the interest in baseball was beginning to dwindle.

Then, in 1964, the Dillon Raceway opened, and some of the players, such as Jimmy Renfrow, turned to stock car racing. But 1962 was the glory year for the Red Legs. Lloyd showed me a trophy that the Red Legs won that year for winning the league championship that he said was one of his most valued possessions. He told me the story of the night they went to Bladenboro to play for the league championship. It had been a long season, and some of the players had dropped out. He said they got to Bladenboro and were getting ready to play when he discovered that none of the pitchers had showed up.

The players had to furnish their own transportation, and he never knew how many might show up. Lloyd said he thought to himself that they had come down to the final game and he had no one to pitch. He got the team together and told them they had no pitcher. Ansel Tyndall, who had pitched a little, said he would pitch, but Lloyd said he needed him to catch because he was their best catcher.

All of a sudden the second baseman, Robert Peele, said that he would pitch. Lloyd said he was a little reluctant, but he didn't have much choice, and as far as he knew, Robert Peele had never pitched a game in his life. The Red Legs went to bat first, and the first five batters all hit doubles to give the Red Legs a good head start. When Robert Peele went to the mound, he had no problem getting the ball over the plate, but he would hardly break a window as slow as he was throwing the ball.

Ansel Tyndall said the opposing team had gotten frustrated from getting behind in the bottom of the first and that they were trying to "kill" the ball in hopes of getting an extra base hit, but they were missing the ball or hitting easy pop flies. The Dillon Red Legs went on to win the game and the championship with a man who had never pitched before.

In talking to a lot of the fellows who played Border Belt ball, they always talked about different people who would attend most all of the games to see them play, and that meant so much to them. Coach Lloyd Meekins talked about a certain player who was dating during the time he played for the Dillon Red Legs, and if the player saw his girl in the stands before the game, he knew he was going to have a good night. He always excelled when she was there. They later married and had many wonderful years together. I am also thankful that many of these men are still alive to read this story, and when I talked to a lot of them, they would remember certain things that might have happened at a certain game and would share the story with me. It would be impossible to list each instance, but I heard some very good stories.

Border Belt baseball has been gone for over forty years, but it still lives in the hearts of some men from their late eighties to their sixties. The Dillon Red Legs continued on until 1965 and were still being managed by Lloyd Meekins. A lot of players came through the Red Legs organization in the time that it existed, and teams came and went through the league. Darlington came into the league in 1963, and also Lake View and Fair Bluff came back, but I have not been able to find the exact specifics.

From what information I could find, Dillon wound up second in the league in 1963. Whiteville remained a strong team during that season and may have won the title. One very interesting article I found was about a game with Lumberton on August 2, 1963. The Lumberton team had a 1–0 lead going into the ninth inning. Carl Hyatt walked and Jack Lee Morrison doubled to tie the score. Harold Grice sacrificed Morrison to third, and Curtis Jones hit a two-run homer to give Dillon the win 3–1. The amazing thing about this game was that Harold Grice pitched all the way for the Red Legs, allowing two hits and striking out twenty Lumberton batters, just one short of the league record.

1963 Dillon Red Legs. *Front with bat*: Mickey Meekins. *Kneeling, left to right*: Jimmy Jackson, Richard "Monkey" Christmas, Jimmy Sawyer, Bill Miller, Bobby Price and Vernon Grimsley. *Standing*: A.Z. Britt Sr., Pete Price, Gene Hayes, Skeeter Hayes, Frank Price, Rembert Cook, Boyd Herring and Coach Lloyd Meekins. *Courtesy of A.Z. Britt.*

There are a lot more players I need to mention who played for the Red Legs, and if anyone is left out, I sincerely apologize; it will be simply because I didn't know about them. Leroy Vaughan was a baseball coach for Lake View and pitched some for the Red Legs. Buddy Rouke came from Charleston and pitched for the Red Legs. Buddy married Joyce Pate and operated Pate's Cleaners for many years. Raymond Pate came from McColl and pitched for the team.

Bill Miller was also a pitcher for the Dillon team. Harold Gasque, who was an outstanding pitcher for Latta High School, said he pitched a little for the Red Legs. Roy Hulon played in the outfield for the team; he is now deceased. J.W. Bailey, who operates a convenience store on Highway 301 South, played some for the Red Legs.

Vernon Grimsley played a good bit of first base for the team and, as I understand, managed the team the last year that it operated. I haven't been able to get in touch with Vernon, but I think the team was called the Astros at that time. Jimmy Jackson played some shortstop for the Red Legs, and another fellow of whom I think a lot, Gene Hayes, played some second base. Gene is a retired truck driver.

Curtis Jones was from Bennettsville and played a lot of baseball. He played Legion Ball, played for the Red Legs and went on to play for the University of South Carolina. The late Pete Price, who became a large farmer, played right field for the team. Some other people who played with the Red Legs were Jimmy Sawyer, Bobby Price, Rembert Cook, Boyd Herring and Lonnie Turner, a man who has done an awful lot for all kinds of sports in the Dillon community. He played some second base, as well as calling the play by play on the PA system.

Red Lanier, a former highway patrolman from Dillon, played some very good baseball with the Red Legs. Red went on to be a top man with the South Carolina Highway Patrol and is now retired in Columbia. Mickey Meekins was the batboy for the Red Legs.

The umpires came out of Fort Bragg and were the only ones who were paid for their services. There are a lot of people I need to thank for their help on this story, such as L.E. "Gabby" Norris, Stacey Griffin, Kromer Stephens, Van Benson, Lloyd Meekins, Jimmy Meekins, Herbert Meekins and all those who furnished photos and other information on this article. And I would like to say a special thank-you to Mr. Lide Miller for his help on this story.

Life on a Tobacco Farm

This is a story of life coming up on a farm, with the emphasis on tobacco farming. I was born and raised on a tobacco farm, and even though I worked on the farm from the time I was probably seven years old, I didn't realize all the aspects of farming and just how much time and effort went into raising a crop of tobacco. I remember how hard the work was because at the time I was on the farm, most all the work was done by hand or with very little of the mechanized means of farming that are used today.

In this story, I will attempt to take you back to the early days of tobacco farming and compare them to the more mechanized ways that a crop is grown today. Before I begin this chapter, I would like to thank those who have been around a little longer than myself and have actually farmed tobacco in past times for their input on this article.

Tobacco has been grown in this area for a very long time, even when Dillon County was part of Marion County. In 1909, cotton was still king of all crops. In 1909, there were over 50,000 acres of cotton planted in Dillon County compared to only 3,300 acres of tobacco. By 1929, cotton had fallen to 40,000 acres and tobacco had jumped to over 10,000 acres.

All crops were very labor intensive in that time, and today it would be impossible to farm as in the old days because of the lack of labor. In the early days, 75 percent of the people in the county lived on farms, and only 25 percent lived in the towns in the county. Today that number has

A Dillon County tobacco field. *Photo by Helen Lane Wiggins.*

reversed; many people live outside town, but these folks are not involved in farming. I don't know the exact numbers, but I would dare say that less than 10 percent are actually engaged in farming.

Farming is big business now and requires a large investment of land and money to operate these farms. I heard a man who I think would be in the know say a few weeks back that at one time there were five hundred tobacco farmers in Dillon County; now there are only five. In the late twenties and thirties, only 18 percent of the landowners did their own farming while less than 1 percent were overseers and 81 percent were tenant farmers or sharecroppers.

Tenant farmers would work a portion of the land, usually about twenty acres, or what was known as a "two- or three-horse farm." When the prices for tobacco began to bring more money for the crop than cotton, many people began to grow more tobacco. On the opening day of the tobacco markets in Dillon in 1919, the price for the weed brought a whopping twenty-one cents per pound. Over 200,000 pounds were sold on opening day. Needless to say, the tenants needed a large family to work their crops.

Life on a Tobacco Farm

The landowners would furnish the tenants with the land, a house to live in and the necessary seeds and fertilizer to grow the crops, as well as cash advances for the tenant to live on during the growing seasons. Usually when the crops were harvested and sold, there was very little, if any, left for the tenant. It was a way of life and about the only way these folks had to make a living, as poor as it was.

Cotton had been overplanted for years, and tobacco seemed to be a crop that the farmer could plant and make a decent return for his investment. In time, tobacco would come to be known as the Golden Leaf, and many tobacco farmers would make a good living growing the so-called weed. Maybe you have heard the statement made that most anybody could farm, but I beg to differ with this statement. Even though many farmers may had little education back at that time, I consider farming a very complicated life. A lot of the know-how may have been passed down from generation to generation, but just anybody could not go out and raise a crop. It took a lot of patience, very hard work and a lot of luck to make a good crop. In this story, I will attempt to take you with the best of my ability through the raising of a crop of tobacco.

We will start with the gathering of fuel with which to cure the tobacco, and in the twenties to the early forties that was done with wood. In the fall after the crop was gathered and sold, the task was to gather wood to cure the next crop. The farmers went out into the woods and cut trees. The trees had to be a certain size to fit the furnace at the curing barn. The wood was cut with a crosscut saw, which required two persons. There were no power saws at that time, and the saws had to be sharpened regularly to get a good cut on the wood.

The trees were cut in about five-foot lengths to fit the furnace and were carried to the barn by a two-horse wagon. Hard wood was used because it burned longer and provided more heat. The wood was stacked at the barn to dry before using. Many cords of wood would have to be cut to last during the curing season. Keep in mind that the wood was loaded and unloaded by hand and stacked very neatly in rows in order to have easy access to fire the furnace.

Next was the job of preparing the tobacco beds where the tobacco plants would be grown to use for the tobacco crop. The beds were plowed and prepared to plant the tobacco seed. Beds were planted before Christmas.

The beds were probably thirty yards long and fifteen to eighteen feet wide, and poles were placed around the beds on which to place the cheesecloth cover to keep the plants from freezing. A site for the beds was usually near a patch of woods, which would provide a windbreak for the beds. When the farmer would cut his cotton stalks in the fall, these stalks would be placed on the beds, sometimes several feet high, and burned to provide a base to plant the tiny tobacco seeds. If you have ever seen a tobacco seed, you know they are very small, about the size of a mustard seed.

You could plant about five beds with just an ounce of tobacco seed. The seed had to be very carefully planted just under the earth, because if they were planted too deep they would not come up. Some people mixed the seed with a substance like cornmeal in order to sow the seed on the bed. After the seed was planted, the bed was raked with a yard rake just to cover a small amount of dirt over the seed.

Then the cheesecloth cover was placed over the beds with stakes placed every so many feet to keep the cover off the plants as they began to grow. The tiny plants would begin to grow in about thirty days, but when the plants came up the weeds would come up as well. The weeds would have to be pulled by hand, which I recall was a very tedious job, in order to know the tobacco from the weeds and not pull the wrong thing. Boards were placed across the beds to sit on so you did not get on the plants. It was a very slow and tiresome job.

The beds were usually weeded about three times before the plants would be ready to set out. Now, the plants are grown in a hothouse by the grower or they just buy their plants from someone who specializes in just the growing of the plants. This requires a lot more investment but much less labor.

Next we get into the preparing of the land to plant the tobacco; I am talking about the days before tractors were used and all the plowing was done with horses or mules. There was a hand plow, what we would call a bottom plow today, which was a plow that ran deep into the ground that would turn the earth over in a fashion that would get rid of any roots from a previous crop and break the land well to have a good crop. With a one-horse plow, a good man could break an acre or maybe a little more on a long day; a two-horse plow could break two acres a day. With the tractors and plows of today, a farmer can break that much in a matter of a few minutes.

Life on a Tobacco Farm

Tobacco plant bed and Mary Elizabeth B. Usher Crosland pulling plants. *Courtesy of Lucille Berry Easterling.*

We have just gotten started on raising a crop of tobacco. Before we continue with the steps of growing tobacco, I would like to point out that tobacco could not be grown just anywhere. Tobacco is only grown in the Pee Dee area of South Carolina, which of course is in the most northeastern part of the state. Tobacco must have a very fertile soil in which to grow, and as we move into the upstate, we see very little tobacco grown because the land is not suited for that crop.

You will find the same thing in North Carolina: only the eastern part of that state grows tobacco. Northern Florida, southern Georgia and lower Virginia also grow tobacco, but there again in certain areas. Tobacco is grown in some other states as well, but this tobacco is a different type of tobacco called burly tobacco.

I guess a lot of folks wonder with so many health issues about tobacco just why I would be doing this article on tobacco. When our ancestors began growing tobacco many years ago, they didn't know that tobacco was harmful to one's health and all they were trying to do was support their families. Tobacco became a crop with which they could make a decent return for their investment after the demand for cotton began to dwindle.

Now we return to the crop, as the farmer was getting the land ready to plant the tobacco. The stalks had been cut and the land was disked and plowed to turn over to make ready for the crop. The next step was to make rows in which to plant the tobacco. It was called "running the rows." This was another painstaking job.

With mules and another type of plow, a man would set up two stakes in the field, both completely in line, and it would be his job to try and run these rows as straight as possible. It used to amaze me just how straight these rows would be when he finished.

Today it is a lot easier to get this job done. It is easier to control a tractor than a hardheaded mule that would want to go the opposite way from what you wanted. The rows were run in March, and the tobacco would be ready to set out in April or the first of May. The plants would have be very carefully pulled from the beds and carried in a bucket or small tub to the field.

In the very early times, the tobacco was planted by using a wooden peg with a sharp end to make a hole in the bed of the rows and the plant would be placed in the hole. Then with your foot you would press the soil around the plant. The plants had to be so many inches apart to give them room to grow. Water had to be carried to the field to water the plants. When you finished a day of planting tobacco in this manner, there was a good chance you would have a very sore back.

The first means of setting tobacco mechanically was called a hand transplanter. This was a device about three feet in length that was pointed at one end and had two compartments to it. The larger side held water, and a smaller tube was where you would drop a plant. When you used the pointed end to make the hole, by pressing a trigger the plant and an amount of water would be released. This was much less trouble than having to bend over to set each plant.

Just a few years later, the horse-drawn planters were made where two people could ride the planter and drop the plants at the same time. Today, many acres can be planted in one day compared to being able to plant maybe one acre in the old days. When the tobacco was set out, the first thing you worried about was a late freeze. If this happened, you had to replant the damaged plants.

Life on a Tobacco Farm

Setting out tobacco with a hand setter. *Courtesy of Lucille Berry Easterling.*

Once the plants took root and began to grow, you had to fertilize the plants. This was done at that time with a mule- or horse-drawn tool that looked like a plow in appearance but had a distributor on the frame that held the fertilizer. There was a gear that turned and released the fertilizer to the plants.

Of course then you had the problems of weeds choking out the plants, so the tobacco would have to be hoed about three times during the growing process. After hoeing, the tobacco would have to be plowed; first a plow moved the soil away from the bed, causing a bed in the middle of the furrow, and then a middle buster plow was used to throw the soil back onto the beds. This had to be done several times during the growing season. Today, there are chemicals used that pretty much control all weeds. In my opinion, farming is a science, and even back then if you didn't work at a crop there would be very little product to harvest.

When the tobacco plants began to grow, you had the insects to worry about. First would come the budworms, a small worm that could do a lot of damage to the plant. In the old days, they were poisoned with the use

Spraying tobacco for worms. *Courtesy of Lucille Berry Easterling.*

of a piece of knit cloth that you would fill with poison and shake over the plant to kill the budworms. Later on, you had the dreaded tobacco worm or hornworm. This was a large green worm that could eat its weight in tobacco leaf in just a short period of time. Both of these worms were laid by moths, and in the case of the hornworm, a farmer would get his children into the field and they would physically pull these nasty-looking worms off the leaves and kill them with a stick. These worms would always be on the underside of the leaf, so you had to look for them.

Also during the growing season, you had the "suckers" to worry about when the plant was almost matured. The sucker was like another plant that would begin to grow between the tobacco leaves. If these suckers were not broken off, they would hinder the growth of the plant. This was a very hard and tedious job.

Again today, there are chemicals that take care of all that. I have often wondered if it was the chemicals or the tobacco that harmed our health. Today there are tractors with large tires that will run over the tops of the plants without damaging the plants and will spray several rows at one time. The last thing to be done before the crop is harvested is to "top" the plant. As the plant grows larger, it produces a flower at the top of the plant. This flower has to be broken off by hand to keep it from stunting the growth of the plant.

And, of course, the biggest foe the farmer had to face and still does today is the weather. There is danger of too little rain, too much rain, hail, strong winds and a drought. This is one thing the farmer has no control over whatsoever; it is all in God's control. When a farmer plants a crop, he has no idea how things may turn out; all he can do is pray that God will bless his crop.

The idea was to make as many pounds of the leaf as possible, because tobacco was sold by the pound. Back then if a farmer could make 1,000 or 1,200 pounds per acre he was doing pretty well. In later times, the yield was much more, and eventually a farmer was only allowed to make so many pounds.

Well, by now it is around the Fourth of July, and it is time to start harvesting the tobacco, which we called "putting in." By this time, the stems on the lower stalk were beginning to ripen, and it was very important to harvest only the bottom leaves on which the stems were ripe enough to cure out. The very bottom leaves were called "sand lugs," and they were the worst to harvest because you had to bend down so much. These leaves were also usually very dirty because they touched the ground. Today, these leaves are not even used; they are just taken off and thrown away.

The men and older boys usually did the "cropping of the leaves." In some areas it was called "priming" and some called it "pulling." Folks, many of you I realize have never cropped sand lug tobacco, and believe me you haven't missed a thing. This had to be about the hardest, hottest, dirtiest work that a person has ever done. When you have cropped tobacco on a July or August day when the temperature is about ninety-five degrees and the sweat mixed with tobacco gum is running in your eyes and you look down the row and see the heat waves moving up and down and you don't get any breeze in a tobacco field, believe me, you get tough very quick.

Most men worked barefoot, and the dirt would be so hot on your feet that it was almost unbearable. You looked forward to getting to the end of the row, where if you were lucky you could catch a little bit of breeze.

Water was brought to the field in buckets maybe two or three times a day to drink so the men would not get dehydrated. I have experienced headaches, cramps and some nausea from the extreme heat in a tobacco field. I never had to leave the field, but I have seen men have to leave for a shaded area.

There used to be a saying about the heat. We called it the "monkey." I remember men asking, "Did you bring your peanuts today, because the monkey is going to be after you" or "the monkey is on your back." I started cropping tobacco when I was about twelve or thirteen, and you sure grew up fast on a tobacco farm. I think the thing I remember most about cropping tobacco was the tobacco gum from the leaves. This gum was a black substance that would build up on your hands and arms, and it was very hard to get off.

By the time tobacco season was over, you had a good suntan and your feet were tough as nails. You made the sum of forty cents an hour for your time if you worked for someone else, but if you were working your own tobacco, you got nothing until the crop was sold, if you were lucky.

You cropped about three leaves from a stalk, or what was ripe. When you got an armload, you placed them in a drag, which was a rectangular box affair about eight feet long made of wood with wooden glides on the bottom that was pulled by a mule down a wide empty row called a "drag row." The drag was usually driven by a young boy of seven to twelve years old. I have done my share of that, too. This job would make you a whopping thirty cents an hour. Later, tractors were used to pull the flatbed drags.

It wasn't too bad a job, until you got a mule that had a mind of its own and decided to turn the drag over and tear down several stalks of tobacco. This is not a problem today when the tobacco is harvested by a mechanical harvester that folks can ride on and can harvest more in a day than eight men could do back then.

The tobacco would be taken to the curing barn by the drag boy and his faithful mule. I worked some mules that I literally hated and would like to have killed them if I could have gotten away with it. If you have never had a big, hot, sweaty, stinking mule relieve himself right in your face on a hot day, then you are very fortunate.

When the drag reached the barn—which in that time had a shelter and benches built around it—the drag was unhooked from the mule and then hooked to an empty drag. The full drag would be unloaded usually by an older person who was not able to work in the fields anymore. He or she would take armloads of tobacco to the benches and place it where the women were, who would hand several leaves at a time to the person who would "string" the tobacco.

Most of the barn help were women, and the stringer was an important job. Her job was to string the tobacco on what was called a "tobacco stick" that would be placed in a hole on the back of the bench. This was done with "tobacco twine," and it was very important not to string too many leaves at a time or to string it too tight; if so, the tobacco would not cure out properly. There would be two women or girls who would hand the tobacco to the stringers. When the stick was full, the person who "toted sticks" would take the sticks into the barn and hang them on the bottom tiers. Barn help was paid less than field help. At the noon hour, everybody would stop for dinner; we didn't eat lunch back then.

Green tobacco on sticks ready for barn curing. *Courtesy of Lucille Berry Easterling.*

The women would head to the house to finish up the meal that had been started before daylight that morning. The biscuits or corn bread would still have to be cooked, and the iced tea would have to be made, if you had any ice. It was sort of customary to take a couple of hours off during that time and rest up before going back to the fields.

The hired help would eat what they brought from home or go to the nearest store and get a cinnamon bun and a slice of bologna or maybe a slice of hoop cheese. All this, along with a big orange or grape drink, would set you back about fifty cents. Some might prefer to dine on sardines or a can of pork and beans. You see, we folks on the farm had not heard of a forty-hour workweek and time and a half for overtime, and the minimum wage was not even thought of. If you were lucky enough to get a generous farmer, he might send to the store and provide you with a "cold drink" sometimes during the day.

So you think the tobacco season is about over—hardly. Next we get into curing the tobacco and getting it ready for market. We have started harvesting the crop and the tobacco leaves have been sent to the curing barn to be strung onto tobacco sticks and placed in the barn to be cured. As we have mentioned, the men and boys usually did the work in the fields and the women would do the work at the barn.

The barns in that time were built of wood, and many times they would be made from logs. The barns were usually of a square design, and I don't remember the dimensions, but they were about twenty feet square. The floor was dirt and the roof was tin, and the barns were tall in design. There were two doors, one on each side of the barn, and a small window near the top that was used to check the tobacco while it was curing. Inside the barn were many tier poles that were made for the sticks of tobacco to hang on while curing. The barns were about twenty feet tall, and the sticks would be hung all the way to the top.

There was a brick furnace where the barn was fueled from outside the barn. The heat would travel through pipes that were called flues. These flues were arranged around the inside the barn so the heat would be distributed all over the barn.

When the men finished gathering the tobacco from the field, they would come to the barn to hang the sticks to be cured. This was another important job because the sticks needed to be just the right distance apart so the tobacco would cure evenly. If the stems did not cure out properly, this would lower the price of the tobacco. Hanging the tobacco, which would start in the top of the barn, would take a pretty spry young man to balance himself on two of the tier poles without falling. It was a fairly dangerous job, and people have gotten broken bones from falling from the top of the barn.

I remember standing on the dirt floor and hoisting the sticks to the man who was hanging, and the man on the bottom usually got all the dirt in his eyes. This could be a pretty rough job also when the temperature was ninety degrees or higher. Now that I think about it, there were no easy jobs in farming tobacco.

After the barns were filled came perhaps the most important part of the tobacco crop, and that was curing the tobacco. This was usually done by the father in the family or one of the more experienced family members because it took a lot of knowledge. When it was time to "fire" the barn, as it was called, the wood that was gathered during the winter was placed in the furnace and the curing process began. The fire was started out as a low heat and was slowly worked up to a higher temperature. Now, there were no thermostats on the heating systems back then; the heating process was all a matter of knowledge. When you needed more heat, you simply added more wood.

During the curing time, the farmer would almost live at the barn. The heat had to be checked constantly, and there was always the chance of fire inside the barn if leaves fell on the flues. A lot of tobacco barns burned back then. The person curing the tobacco usually spent the night at the barn to keep watch over the tobacco because one barn lost could take away any profit he might make that year. The heat was checked often by a thermometer that hung inside the door through a small glass in the door. You did not want the temperature to drop rapidly inside the barn, as could be caused by a thunderstorm. If so, this would cause the "green" to set into the tobacco.

I remember the smell of tobacco curing in the barn; it was a pleasant smell that I enjoyed. When the barn finished curing, the tobacco was removed form the barn. This was called "taking out," just like "putting in," and the tobacco was taken to a pack house. This is where another big job came in, and that was getting the leaf ready for market. Before

I get into that process, I would like to mention that sometimes during the growing season the tobacco would ripen so fast that it would have to come out of the fields or it would be damaged from the sun. If a farmer had only one barn, this became a problem.

I remember helping an uncle with his crop one year when his tobacco ripened so fast that we had to get up at three o'clock in the morning to take a barn out and turn right around and go to the fields about six o'clock and put another barn right back in. This made for a very long day. There wasn't very much playtime during this time.

Getting back to preparing the crop for market, in that time the tobacco had to be graded and tied into "bats" to be sold at the markets. The grading was done by a person who was experienced in tobacco in order to recognize what leaf needed to be put in a certain grade. The buyers would not buy the leaf unless it was graded correctly. If I remember, there were about four grades: first grade, second grade, green and trash grade.

Every leaf was sold for some price. Back then, the green or trash might bring ten cents per pound. For that reason, the farmer could not afford to have very much of these grades. As the tobacco was taken off the sticks, the grader would sort the leaves into piles of the different grades. Then the persons who would tie the tobacco would gather about the amount they could put their fingers around. They would wrap the tie leaf—a smooth, flexible leaf—around the stems, which had to be very level, and pull the stem back through the handful of tobacco. Thus was made a bat of tobacco. The bats were then placed on a "grading stick" so the tobacco was easier to handle. This made it easy to lay the tobacco neatly into a tobacco basket at the market or before leaving home. This made the leaf more attractive to the buyers. A great part of the grading and tying was done by women.

Sometime in the 1960s, perhaps the greatest labor-saving process was instituted when the tobacco companies started buying loose leaf tobacco. This eliminated all this grading and tying of tobacco.

A lot of farmers would treat their help and families to a fish fry when harvesting season was over. This would usually be held at the tobacco barn, and the fish would be cooked in an iron wash pot. The children would have a big time playing games, and the adults would sit and talk about whether they would make any money that year. As in that day, farming still depends on a lot of things to have a successful year. Now we will talk about taking the crop to market. During this story I have tried to take you though the steps of raising a crop of flue-cured tobacco. The time of year is now in August, and the Georgia markets have been open for a week and now the time comes for the Pee Dee–area markets to open in North Carolina and South Carolina. A lot of farmers now have tobacco ready to go to market, but there are many who still have a lot to do before they can get their leaf to market.

During the early to middle 1950s, I remember that there were three tobacco warehouses operating in Dillon. There was the Big Tin, which was operated by the Bethea brothers, Vic and Tom Sr. There was the Pee Dee, which was operated by Duncan Dew, Gentry Rogers and Frazier Miller. And there was the Main Street warehouse located where Carl's Food Center is now located, but that warehouse burned in the early fifties. In earlier times there were more markets in Dillon, but I don't have the exact locations and names of these warehouses.

Mullins was the largest market in South Carolina, which if I remember correctly had some twelve warehouses at the time. Fairmont, North Carolina, had a large market, and a lot of the Dillon County farmers sold in Fairmont. There were also markets in Lake City, Darlington, Loris and Conway. The farmer had to make an appointment to sell his tobacco so he could be sure there would be available space at the warehouse.

When the day came to sell the tobacco, it was a big day in the life of the farmer. The tobacco was loaded early on wagons, trailers and trucks for folks who were fortunate enough to have a truck. Going to the market was a big day; the farmer would finally get some money for the hard work that had been going on for several months. Another thing that lay heavy on the mind of the farmer would be just what his tobacco would bring.

There was a government support price on the tobacco at this time, but the hope was that it would bring more. This was before loose-leaf sales, and the tobacco was put in baskets and displayed very nicely to entice the buyers. There was a limit as to how many pounds could be placed in a basket.

I always enjoyed going to the market. It was a time of excitement, and the market would be all abuzz with conversation and people scurrying about making last-minute preparations before the sale started. When the

Unloading cured tobacco. *Courtesy of Lucille Berry Easterling.*

sale started, a warehouseman would lead the sale, and then would come the auctioneer, another warehouseman, the man who marked the ticket and several buyers who lined up on each side of the row of tobacco. The warehouse was allowed to sell only so many piles a day

Before the sale began, a government grader would pull several bats from a pile and mark a grade on the ticket; this is what the buyers would look for in making their bid. When the sale started, the warehouseman leading the sale made the opening bid and the auctioneer would start his chant. The tobacco auctioneer was a very highly skilled job; the auctioneer had to be able to watch all the buyers at one time. A lot of the buyers would never make a sound but would simply wink or make some kind of motion that the auctioneer would have to recognize.

I must admit I could never follow the auctioneer, but I guess you had to see a lot of tobacco sold to be able to know what was going on. When a pile was sold and the auctioneer called the name of the company, the ticket marker would write the price and buyer on the ticket. Needless to say, a lot of farmers would be happy, while some would feel that their tobacco did not bring the price it deserved. A farmer could "turn the

Life on a Tobacco Farm

ticket" on his tobacco and try selling it at another time. After the sale was over and all the tickets were turned in, the farmer made his way to the office to collect his money. This office would have several workers who would add the tickets and then check them again to be sure that the prices were correct. Then the farmer would get a check for the portion of tobacco he had sold that day.

Finally, he would begin to get some of his investment back for the many months of hard work. It would not be until all his crop was sold that he could determine whether he had made any money for his year's work. To show you how tobacco escalated in price over the years, on opening day in 1935, the average price was $23.00 per hundred pounds, and prices were expected to go to $40.00 to $50.00 per hundred. On opening day in the year 2000, when tobacco had been sold loose leaf for many years, it was just tied in sheets; the opening average on the Mullins market was $1.65 per pound.

Reworking tobacco at the warehouse. *Courtesy of Lucille Berry Easterling.*

It was in the middle 1930s that tobacco began to bring a decent price; it went from twelve dollars per hundred in 1933 to over forty dollars in 1935. Today, all the tobacco warehouses are gone and the farmer deals directly with the tobacco companies. The tobacco is sold in bales, without all the preparation that was taken in olden times. I don't have to tell you that tobacco is a dying crop with all the health issues facing tobacco in this day and time. I am not going to get into the health issues because I couldn't explain them anyway.

I would say that there must be some truth in the harm that tobacco causes, but what I have tried to do in this story is to tell you about a way of life that sustained our farmers for many years. I hold no blame toward the farmers whatsoever for any health problems, because when tobacco began to be grown in this part of the country they certainly didn't realize that any of this would come about. They were simply trying to find a way of making a living for their families.

Regardless of what you may think about tobacco today, tobacco fed and housed many of our families over the years. A lot of doctors, lawyers, teachers and many other professions, including ministers, were educated with tobacco money.

I had an appointment with a prominent doctor about two years ago in Florence, and when I went into his office, I could hardly believe what I saw. On the walls were pictures of tobacco scenes, and to my amazement, he still had a smoking section in his office. When he came in to see me, I commented that you certainly didn't see much of this anymore. He answered me by saying, "If it had not been for tobacco, I would not be a doctor today."

I again would like to thank the ones who helped on this article. I especially thank Lucille Easterling for ideas and pictures from a book she published in 2005 called *A Farm Girl's Story*. Some might say, "Just why did you include this story in your book?" It is my opinion that very soon, tobacco will be a forgotten crop in this area; there are young people who have no idea what growing a crop of tobacco is all about. Someday, someone might pick up this book and find another chapter in the *Hidden History of Dillon County*.

Hog-Killing Time

When I walk into one of our supermarkets and gaze at the fine cuts of meat available for us to buy—such as the trays of pork chops all cut so nice and even, the varieties of fresh and smoked ham, some even sliced already so we don't have to cut it—it takes me back in time to when things were not so convenient. I think back to a time when we raised our own pork on the farm, and when the weather began to turn cold in the fall of the year, I remember what was known as hog-killing time. I was raised on the farm, and I guess next to chicken, pork was our most used meat. We had a small family, and we didn't butcher but maybe two hogs a year, which would see us through the year.

Mr. D.W. Bethea owned the farm we lived on, and he raised a lot of hogs for resale during the year. This was before the days of hog farms as we know them now, and my father would see to the welfare of the pigs when they were born and as they grew to the size when they could be sold. Every year, Mr. Bethea would give my dad a couple of small pigs that would be raised in a pen behind our house. When the cold weather came, the pigs would be large enough, perhaps about two hundred pounds, to kill and process for eating.

There are not many people who raise hogs for self-consumption anymore, and if they do, the hogs are taken to a place that will completely process the pork, all neatly cut, wrapped and labeled. Then they take the meat home and put it in a freezer. We didn't have freezers back then,

Elias Maynor and his butchered hogs. *Courtesy of K. Blake Tyner.*

so the meat was salt cured or smoked to keep from spoiling and kept in smokehouses. The hogs had to be killed in cold weather so the meat would not spoil before the salt could cure the meat out. Today, hogs are raised in hog parlors by farmers who do this for a living. Hogs today can be raised to selling size in just a few weeks; in older times it would take a year to get a hog large enough to butcher.

There was nothing easy about raising hogs to eat. The pigs would be placed in a pen made of what we called hog wire. They were not fed in the manner that hogs raised in a hog parlor are raised today. About two months before the hogs were killed, they were moved to a smaller floored pen where they would be fed corn or ground corn with nutrients to get rid of the bitter taste and to produce more fat for the lard that would be produced from the hog. When it came time to kill the hogs, it would usually be a family affair. I had an uncle on my mother's side who would come with his family and help with the

Hog-Killing Time

The hogs are loaded and carried to the slaughterhouse. *Courtesy of Mary Lois Clark.*

processing of the hogs, and then when he killed his hogs, we would go and help him.

The day would start very early. The first thing was to boil water, which was done in large cast-iron pots that were also used for washing clothes. The water had to be very hot in order to loosen the hair on the hog so it would be easy to scrape off. While the water was boiling, the job of killing the hogs was done. My father would take a .22-caliber rifle and shoot the hog in the head, and then he would take an axe and hit him in the head with the blunt end. Then his throat was cut so that he would bleed. The children were usually not allowed to witness this part of the job.

This was not a job for the weak at heart, but this was a matter of being able to eat during the year. After the hog was killed, the men would drag him to a fifty-gallon drum that was buried in a slanted position so it was easier to get the hog in the drum. The drum was about half filled with boiling water. The hog was placed in the drum and turned several times to loosen the hair. A dull knife was used to scrape the hair from the hog to keep from cutting the skin. After scraping the hair from the hog, the heel strings were exposed and the hog was hung from a single tree, which was a tool that was used in plowing a mule. The hog was then hung on a thick board nailed to a tree; it usually took two or three good men to handle this task.

At this time, the remaining hair was scraped from the hog, and then the real skill started when the hog was butchered. A very sharp knife was used to split the front of the hog open, and the inside parts were emptied into a #3 tin tub. For you folks who might not know, there was nothing wasted about the hog. The lungs (which were referred to as lights), the liver, the intestines (which were used for stuffing sausage and liver pudding)—literally everything was used. These inside parts were cooked pretty quickly to prevent spoiling. Sometimes the lights and part of the liver were used to cook what was called liver hash, which was served over rice. I remember it being good, usually served with corn bread, but I don't know if I could eat it now. To my knowledge, the lungs are no longer sold for consumption. Even the feet were cleaned, boiled and pickled in vinegar.

When the insides were cleaned, the hog was laid on a table, and a sharp axe was used to split the backbone. The hams and shoulders were removed to be cured. The wash pots were now used to hold all the fatty parts to boil to make lard. The lard was very important, as everything that was fried would be done with lard. We didn't have cooking oil back then. The skins were cooked as well to make "cracklings"; today they would be called pork rinds. Have you ever eaten crackling bread? The hard skin would be trimmed off and the meat from the crackling would be cooked in meal like you might see fried corn bread today.

The lean part of the backbone, which today would be mostly pork chops, was fried and used in making the sausage. Some of this tasty pork would be used to make a big pot of backbone and rice. Most everybody had a sausage mill, which was a grinder with blades and a handle. The mill would be attached to a table, and the pieces of pork would be fed into the grinder. There was an attachment that was put on the grinder like a spout that was used to stuff the sausage into the intestines or, for a better word, casings.

The cleaning of the intestines was a real chore and was usually done by the women. A reed was used to run through the intestines, and they had to be washed many times to be sure they were clean. The sausage

Hog-Killing Time

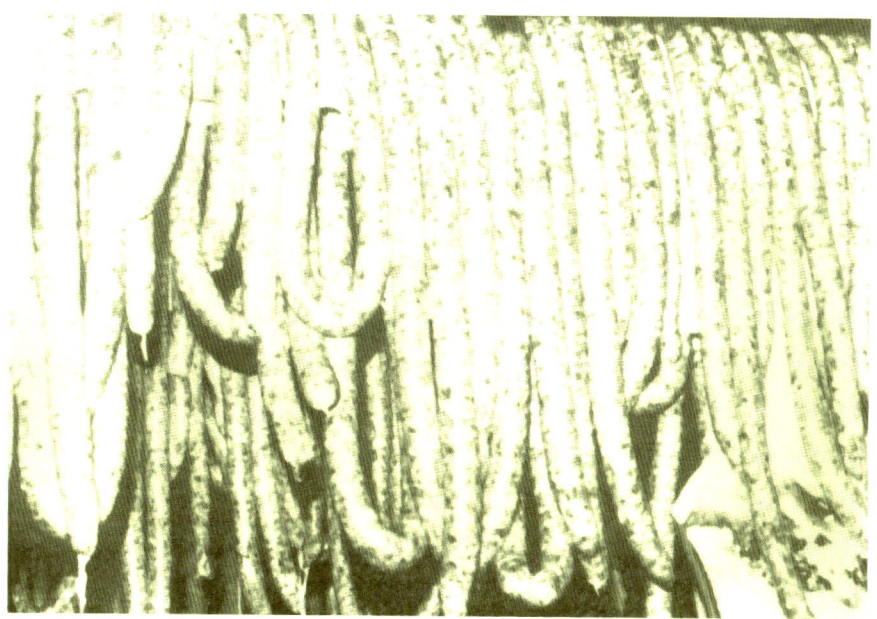

Curing out homemade sausage. *Courtesy of Mary Lois Clark.*

would be seasoned with dried red pepper, sage and other spices to give it a spicy taste. The sausage was then hung in a cool, dry place to cure out. If you have not had a piece of homemade cured sausage, you have missed a lot.

The fatty part of the back would be cut into large wide strips to be made into fatback. This would be salted to cook with vegetables or just fried to eat. The grease from the cooked fatback would be saved to use again for seasoning or frying. As I mentioned, nothing was wasted. The head was boiled until all the meat fell off and was made into souse meat or hog head cheese. This was mixed with different ingredients and had a lot of vinegar in it. The ears were also put into this. When cold, it would form sort of a gel. You can find this sold in stores today.

When the pork was salt cured or smoked, as some would do, you would have some very tasty meat, and when it was cooking, you could smell it for a country mile. I think I will always remember this African American gentleman named Dave Manning walking by our house late one evening about sundown. My mother was cooking some of that "homemade meat," as we called it. We were standing on the back porch, and he called from the road, which was just a few yards away. "Mrs. Wiggins. Do have a biscuit?" She answered, "What do want with a biscuit, Dave?" He said, "I just want to sop some of that air, it smells so good."

Well, things have changed a lot since that time. Now you just walk into a store and pick out about anything you want. If you wonder why we did things like that back then, it was called survival. I will always remember hog-killing time.

Here Comes the Goat Man!

I don't know how many of you will remember anything about the character that this story is about, but I think you might find it interesting even if you never heard of him. Back in 1954, there was a man who came through Dillon traveling on Highway 301. This was before the days of the interstate highways, and he was headed north. Now this was a man like no other I had ever witnessed. I was fourteen years old at the time, and I don't remember how I found out about him or how I got there because I lived several miles away. But I distinctly remember what would become known around Dillon as the "Goat Man."

I guess you would describe him as a dirty Gabby Hayes, a man who used to act in a lot of the old-time western movies. His beard was long, and he wore bib overalls. He wore an old felt hat and brogan shoes, but as strange as he looked was not nearly as strange as the way he traveled. His method of travel was what looked to be a homemade wagon with about every conceivable item you could think of tied to it. If you remember the sitcom *The Beverly Hillbillies*, it looked something like Jed Clampett's truck with no motor.

His wagon was pulled by a team of goats, and he had many goats with him. He had goats of all sizes; the larger ones pulled the wagon, and some were tied to the wagon and ran along beside, while the small goats rode in the wagon. He drew a lot of attention on that night he camped in Dillon. In this day and time we would probably watch the news reporter interview him on TV.

Charles "Ches" McCartney—the "Goat Man." *Courtesy of Don McDowell.*

I remember a lot of people were there to see this strange individual. He camped in a field off Highway 301 South somewhere between the Dillon 301 drive-in theater and what was then Cicero Herring's store. I think the thing I can remember most was the smell. One witness said he saw him coming through Latta, and another said that he stopped at South of the Border. Friends, this was fifty-four years ago, but I never really forgot the Goat Man. He was a topic of conversation around Dillon for a long time, and some developed the term, "You look like the Goat Man." I always wondered about this man, just who he was, where he came from and why he would travel up and down the road with a bunch of goats.

A few weeks back, I was talking with perhaps one of my oldest friends on the telephone. His name is Donald McDowell, and he has lived in the state of Georgia for perhaps the last thirty or more years. He and I were reared just a short ways from each other and attended Latta schools. While we were talking, he asked, "Do you remember the Goat Man?" I told him that I had never forgotten him. He said that there had been a book published about the man and he could probably get me a copy if I wanted it.

I told him that I would love to have a copy of the book. Donald comes back here several times a year to visit family, so during the Christmas

Here Comes the Goat Man!

holidays he brought me a copy of the book. The book is called *America's Goat Man* and was written by a man named Darryl Patton. I read the book and found it to be very interesting and sometimes almost unbelievable. I would like to share with you some of the things I found out about the man who once made a trip through Dillon and left a lasting impression on those who saw him and got to talk with him.

The man whom thousands of people all over the United States got to know as the "Goat Man" was born Charles (Ches) McCartney on July 6, 1901. Ches was born in Keokuk County, Iowa, the son of Albert and Louise McCartney. Iowa was farming country, and that is the profession that he chose in life.

By the time the Great Depression came, McCartney had bought a farm and was doing pretty well for himself. He had married his first wife, and they had a son. During the Depression, things got really bad for the young farmer, and he wound up losing his land and almost everything else he owned. Ches had to take a job with the WPA in order to survive. While working with the WPA, he had the misfortune of having a tree fall across his body. He said that he lay there for hours before he was found. In McCartney's words, he was pronounced dead and his body was taken to the morgue. Lucky for Ches, the undertaker was slow, and by the time the undertaker got to him, he had regained consciousness and the life had come back to his body. He said it was like he had been raised from the dead.

The accident left McCartney with several broken bones and a badly mangled left arm. He was left with a decision to make: should he become a ward of the state and live off public assistance, or was there something else that he could do? He made a decision, and a strange decision it was. He built a four-wheel wagon made with iron wheels.

The only livestock he had left was a few goats. He made gear for the goats to pull the wagon, and he also made a two-wheel wagon to pull behind the larger wagon. This would be the living quarters for the family of three. McCartney loaded everything he had left into the wagon, and in 1936, he started on a journey that would last for the next forty years.

When Ches McCartney left the farm he had lost near Keokuk, Iowa, all he knew was that he had to move off the farm. He had no relatives he could live with or give him a helping hand during this very trying time. Ches had a young wife and one small son.

The Goat Man talks to an interested onlooker. *Courtesy of Don McDowell.*

Ches McCartney loaded everything he owned into that wagon, which appeared to be a rolling junkyard, and left the small cabin he lived in, never to return. A neighbor who lived down the road from McCartney said, "I wonder where that fool thinks he is going in that contraption." I don't think Charles McCartney had any idea as to where he was going, but the itinerant farmer with a second-grade education in time to come would become known to the people of America as simply the "Goat Man."

Not very much is known about McCartney from the time he left Iowa until he wound up in Twiggs County, Georgia, near a small town called Jeffersonville in 1942. His wife had left him not very long after they left Iowa; she said she could not endure the hardships of living on the road under such conditions. McCartney said she ran off with another man. Ches was left with a young son, Albert Gene, to care for.

McCartney bought two acres of land outside Jeffersonville and built a two-room shack. The building never had electricity or running water. You might think he was considering settling down, but that was far from the truth.

For the next thirty years, this unique vagabond would travel the roads of America. This story sometimes seems less than truthful, but there is

Here Comes the Goat Man!

The Goat Man camps for the night. *Courtesy of J.W. Price.*

enough documented evidence to prove that he did much of what I am talking about. He claimed to be married three times and had a total of three children, but the boy Albert Gene is the only one who is mentioned by name. He said the other two wives died of natural causes. No names are mentioned for them.

The Goat Man began to build his popularity in the late forties and early fifties. He became a legend, especially in the southeastern part of the country. He claimed to have traveled in every state except Hawaii and logged over 100,000 miles in his years on the road. I would have some doubt about his traveling to places like Alaska in a wagon pulled by goats, but there is documentation of him being in Indiana, Illinois, Kentucky and some of the other northern states.

I mentioned that I saw him when he passed through Dillon in the year 1954. Some Dillon folks say he came through here more than one time. Dorothy Hunt Neilson, a former resident of Dillon, said she saw the Goat Man on First Avenue near Bill Coward's store in about 1957.

Many stories have been told about the Goat Man over the years. Some say he was a very wealthy man and that he had huge bank accounts in Georgia. Others say that a woman would follow along miles behind him in a new Cadillac and would come to where he was camped late at night. These stories were told everywhere he traveled; everybody had a story about the Goat Man.

In my research of Ches McCartney, I discovered that he lived a life of poverty; his only income was from the sale of picture postcards, made of him and his strange traveling caravan, which he sold for twenty-five cents. He later had a little pamphlet printed about his life. Some folks along the way would bring him some food and maybe give him a dollar or two.

The Goat Man was said to be a self-proclaimed preacher of the gospel. He said that he was licensed by a Pentecostal church someplace in Georgia.

I guess the only way to describe Ches McCartney was that he was a vagabond, always filthy in appearance. His clothes were always greasy, and his face was covered in soot from burning old tires he would find along the road. He smelled just like the goats that he traveled with. He admitted that he would go for years without taking a bath.

There are dozens of statements from people all over who saw and talked to the Goat Man over the years. It got to be that when a town found out that he was coming through, the word would get out and some of the local radio stations and newspapers would make an announcement about his passing through.

It has been reported that as many as three hundred people might show up where he was camped just to get a look at this folklore individual. Most said they couldn't stay very long due to the smell. Many people would show up just to take a picture of this man with the long beard and his goats. Several people said that at times there would be a boy traveling with McCartney, perhaps his son Albert Gene.

The children liked to pet the goats, which I have seen described as many as thirty-five and as few as eighteen. Most reports say that the wagon was pulled by nine or ten of the larger goats, while some of the other goats would follow along behind and, on McCartney's command, would push the wagon with their heads such as when they were going up a hill.

There was also a smaller two-wheel wagon that was pulled behind the larger wagon. This is where the baby goats would ride until they were large enough to walk on their own. It was said that McCartney had a three-legged goat that always rode in the wagon.

Here Comes the Goat Man!

As I worked on this story of the legend of the man who became known as simply the Goat Man, I wondered about the hardships that he must have endured in all those days of his travels. I thought about the extreme heat he endured and the thunderstorms he traveled through.

McCartney told about spending a week on Mount Eagle in Tennessee during a terrible ice storm. He told of huddling up to his goats during the night to keep from freezing to death. His diet consisted of things like a pot of cabbage cooked over an open fire when he stopped for the day.

He said that during his travels he was cursed at by motorists who would be backed up for miles due to his slow-moving caravan. He was not allowed to use public accommodations due to his appearance and the smell of his goats and himself. He said that on a very good day, he might cover as much as twelve miles, and then some days he might not make but three or four miles. This was something that he never worried about, because the Goat Man did not have a schedule or an itinerary to go by. For most of the year, his home was the road.

McCartney had his problems with the highway patrol about his manner of travel and delaying traffic with his slow-moving caravan. I find no instance when he was ever arrested or accused of stealing anything. He picked up all kinds of junk along the way. His wagon was covered with license plates from many different states, and he had reflectors on the back of the wagon so that cars could see the wagon when it began to get dark. I don't find where he traveled very much at night.

A lot of the officers of the highway patrol got used to seeing the Goat Man every so often, and many would try and route him down roads that were not used as much. McCartney lost a lot of goats on the road. Some would get run over by cars, and he also had some stolen while he was sleeping.

One of his best goats was killed by a bow hunter one night, I guess just for the heck of it. He said that perhaps one of his best friends was a goat named Billy who traveled with him for some twenty years. McCartney said these goats were his family and they respected him, unlike some humans who he came across during his travels. It seemed like the goats understood what he said, and he understood them.

He said that he was mistreated a lot of times, like the time when three young hooligans attacked his camp, turned over his wagons, cut his goats

The Goat Man and two of his prized goats. *Courtesy of Don McDowell.*

loose and cut twenty-seven stitches on the side of his head when he tried to fight back. But Ches said that most people treated him decently. Some would offer for him to water his goats at their farms and let them graze in their fields. Some would even prepare food and bring it to him.

Ches McCartney never owned a radio or a television set, but with what little education he had he learned to read a newspaper and was pretty informed on world affairs. In 1959, he announced that he would run for president of the United States, but after having a conversation with John F. Kennedy, he decided not to run. I will let you be the judge of that. He predicted in 1968 that the world would come to an end in three years. So far that hasn't happened either. He predicted that this country would have another depression; maybe this might still happen.

It would probably be impossible in this day for a man like McCartney to travel the distances he claimed to have traveled with the superhighways and the amount of traffic on the road today. A story was told about an instance in Fayetteville, North Carolina, sometime in the 1950s when the traffic was backed up for so many miles on Highway 301 that the highway patrol had to get the Goat Man off the highway and route him

Here Comes the Goat Man!

down a back road. Statements came from all over the country about the Goat Man coming through their town and maybe staying for a day or so. Many people who were children at the time had memories of seeing the Goat Man and maybe talking to him.

As I mentioned, Ches McCartney said he was a minister of the Pentecostal faith. McCartney didn't travel on Sunday, and he was probably not welcomed in many churches, but it was said that every Sunday afternoon, he would pull out his old tattered Bible and preach a little sermon to those who cared to listen. It is this writer's belief that McCartney traveled mostly in the Southeast, even though people from many different states talked about the one and only Goat Man.

In all my research on the Goat Man, the only thing I have not been able to figure out is just why this rather strange man traveled all over this country for some forty years with a small herd of goats. Ches McCartney had his reasons, I guess. One thing I need to clear up is the rumor that spread around to my knowledge sometime about the 1970s that McCartney and most of his goats had been killed when an eighteen-wheeler ran into the back of his strange caravan. This was only a rumor, but it spread by word of mouth around the country.

There are many conflicting stories in the book written about McCartney, but it is my opinion that he ended his travels about 1976 and retired to his little two-room shack located just outside Jeffersonville, Georgia. In my research, this was the only property the man owned. He was seventy-five years old at the time. I found that his son Albert Gene would stay with his father from time to time, but there is not a lot known about the son.

It is my opinion that both the father and son were both mentally impaired to an extent. It was said by local citizens that after his "retirement," Ches McCartney would walk along Highway 80 for miles at a time picking up cans and other discarded items, much as he did in his travels with his goats.

It was also said that McCartney gave most all his goats to a zoo in Florida except for a couple he kept as pets. Someone helped McCartney get a small Social Security check for about sixty-five dollars a month. This was his only income. He never had electricity or running water. In 1978, after having eaten some supper that he had fixed on a cast-iron stove that had cracked from years of use, McCartney fell asleep on his cot. Coals from the heater fell through the crack and set his shack on fire.

When the Goat Man awoke, the house was engulfed in flames. He said he jumped over the flames to get outside, but his beard and hair were singed and he had suffered minor burns. At the age of seventy-seven, Ches McCartney was homeless. Some people in the area helped the Goat Man get an old school bus that was pulled on his land, and for the next ten years that served as his home. During this time, his last goat died, and for the first time in many years Ches McCartney was without one of the animals that he had been so well known for. Ches didn't have many friends due to perhaps the manner in which he lived, but one would certainly have to say that he was a survivor.

In 1987, McCartney suffered frostbite on two of his toes, perhaps from the lack of heat in his school bus home. He was hospitalized, and

Ches McCartney at the Eastview Nursing Home. *Courtesy of Don McDowell.*

Here Comes the Goat Man!

the toes had to be removed. The Twiggs County Department of Family and Children's Services sought admission for McCartney at the Eastview Nursing Home in Macon. He was admitted on a temporary basis, and he always said that he would be going back home shortly. At the nursing home, McCartney probably lived the best life he had ever known. He was clean, his beard was neatly trimmed and he ate on a regular schedule.

When the word got out that Ches McCartney was a resident at the Eastview Nursing Home, many people began to visit him on a regular basis. He would sit and tell them about his travels as the legendary Goat Man. Mind you, none of the stories would be the same. He became somewhat of a celebrity, and folks would come from miles around to hear the old man tell his tales. He tended to exaggerate about his age. He would tell some that he was over 100 years old, sometimes maybe 110.

He found a "girlfriend" at the nursing home, a retired nurse who was a patient there, and McCartney would brag about having a young woman. She was only eighty-five. A local artist named Larry Martin came to the home and drew a sketch of the Goat Man. McCartney signed the sketch, and prints were made and sold of the famed Goat Man.

Darryl Patton interviewed him several times and wrote the book *America's Goat Man*. It is not clear whether Ches McCartney ever received any proceeds from this. Ches McCartney never left Eastview Nursing Home. In 1998, his son Albert Gene was found murdered in the woods behind their school bus home. No details were available on the incident. Five months later, the famed Goat Man, Charles "Ches" McCartney, passed away. He was ninety-seven years old.

Like a lot of people who I might write about, the Goat Man will never be found in history books, but he was a part of history for a lot of regular folks like you and I who will remember this strange individual for perhaps the rest of our lives. He may not have done a lot for society, but he left us with an interesting tale to share with the younger generations. I think maybe he just liked meeting people along the way and the attention he got because he was a little different.

When I wrote this story that was published in the local newspaper, I never dreamed that so many people would remember this strange individual. I received e-mails, letters, phone calls and a lot of personal contact from people who wanted to talk about the Goat Man.

I realize he was not a native of Dillon County, but he left a lasting impression on many people of this area. Many younger people who never saw the Goat Man, but had heard their parents or grandparents talk of the man, said that finally they had learned something about this unique person who traveled the roads of America for some forty years.

The Maple Swamp Gang

This story takes us back in time to the days of the Civil War, when Dillon County was still part of Marion County. As you read this story, there will be things that you may want to consider that may have contributed to it. This account was written by Phillip Yancy Bethea in the year 1916. You will also find accounts of this matter in W.W. Sellers's book, *The History of Marion County.* John S. Murphy recorded some of these events in the strange diary he kept back in the 1800s concerning the days of the Civil War in what is now Dillon County.

I would like to thank Larry Jones, our Dillon County building code enforcement officer, for sharing work that he has done on this time in our history. Larry is a real buff on Civil War history and a staunch member of the Andrew Harllee Sons of the Confederate Veterans unit in Dillon County. I also need to thank Mrs. Mary Mac Stephens, a lady I have learned to admire for her study and knowledge of Dillon County, for her input on this story.

This story begins during the War Between the States. At that time, what we know as our home of Dillon County was upper Marion County. This was long before Dillon was a town and some fifty years before Dillon became a county. At that time there were a lot of people living on Maple Swamp, which began just outside of what is now the town of Dillon going southeast. At that time, there was much more swampland in this area.

This story is about a band of deserters who refused to fight for the South during the war. I would like to point out first of all that some of the names mentioned in this story have or show no reflection on citizens of this county today, and also there were people of the same name who did fight in the war and were heroes in the war against the North.

The group of men who were deserters or avoided service to the South became known as the "Maple Swamp Gang." As this story unfolds, we will see that we really had a war of our own going on right here where many of us live today. To avoid enlistment in the Confederate army, these men took to the swamps for hiding. Their chief strongholds were the Maple Swamp and the morasses and bays of the Little Pee Dee River. Before the war was over, they spread into other parts of upper Marion County and even into the swamps of Marlboro County. At times, some of these men were picked up by the enrolling officers and sent to the front, but in just a short while, they would desert and join their companions back in the swamps.

The deserters lived by robbing the citizens of the community, some of whom were former neighbors. They usually made their raids at night, but as time went by, they became bolder and would rob and destroy in the daytime. They would threaten people who were aiding the local officials by posting notices that anyone who aided in trying to capture them would be killed. They would even mention names of those who were marked for slaughter. The citizens were horrified by this gang, and the men who were not able to fight in the war or were too old began to take steps to fight back against this ruthless gang.

Two divisions of the Home Guard were formed to try to capture or kill this group who was wreaking havoc in the community. Reverend Charles J. Fladger was made captain of one unit, and Colonel Thomas Manning was the leader of the other division. Fladger had served four months in the Confederate army before his wife died and he was sent home to care for his children. Being a preacher, he had seen little time in battle. Some of the members of his unit were Reverend Samuel Bethea, Reverend Joel Allen, Dr. Alfred W. Bethea, John R. Bethea, James R. Bethea, Jesse Bethea and others not mentioned.

The Maple Swamp Gang

Dr. John Jeremiah Bethea fought against the Maple Swamp Gang. *Courtesy of Johnny Rogers, great-great-grandson.*

Bear in mind that all able-bodied men were already serving in the army, so this group was made up mostly of men who were exempt from the war, such as ministers, doctors and young boys or old men. On the other hand, the Maple Swamp Gang was made up of tough, ruthless men who didn't mind killing or being shot at. The main leader of the gang was Arthur Jackson, who was known as "Arder," and his brother John was his right-hand man. Others prominent on the deserter list were Archibald Surles, Levi Surles, Pink Surles, Hugh

P. Price and members of the families of Hyatt, Coward, Herring and many others.

The Home Guard would make occasional raids into the swamps in search of the deserters but with very little success. The gang was a crafty bunch and always seemed to know what the Home Guard had planned. It was believed that they may have had inside information from folks on the outside. On or about November 17, 1864, Sheriff William P. Campbell went into the Maple Swamp section looking for a man who was avoiding arrest. It is believed that this man was a local deserter.

Sheriff Campbell had been warned not to go alone but to take a posse with him. The sheriff did not heed the warning and was able to capture his man. This arrest took place in the present-day vicinity of Dove Mill Road, just a short distance from Tobacco Land Road near the old John A. Dove residence.

Sheriff Campbell was taking his prisoner to the Marion Courthouse. When he neared Campbell's Bridge, he was shot and killed and the prisoner went free. Campbell's Bridge was off present-day Highway 57 behind the old Page farm near Floydale but somewhat farther north than the present location. One reliable source said that Sheriff Campbell was actually killed at his home. This was the beginning of a bloody battle between the Maple Swamp Gang and the local citizens of present-day Dillon County.

From there, things went from bad to worse until after the war ended. In late December, the Home Guard was called out to meet near Donaho Bay (in the Minturn community near Reedy Creek Presbyterian Church). They had been informed that the gang was hiding out in that bay. The guard formed a line of sentinels to surround the bay. During the night, a sentinel reported seeing several deserters carrying a freshly killed hog to their camp in the bay. The next morning, December 28, 1864, it was learned that the premises of a Mr. McDougal had been robbed and a fat hog was killed and carried off. The Home Guard was sure that now they had the gang surrounded and would be able to capture them.

The two leaders of the guard laid plans to attack the deserters. They would send in several squads of men from different directions with plans to meet at the deserters' camp about the same time. What the guard didn't know was that the gang had already anticipated the attack and was

The Maple Swamp Gang

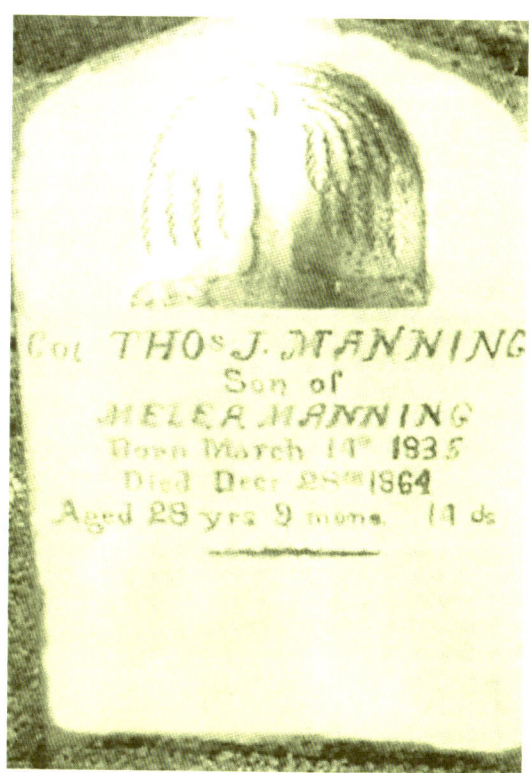

The headstone of Colonel Thomas J. Manning, killed by the Maple Swamp Gang. *Photo by Helen Lane Wiggins.*

lying in wait. When the Home Guard arrived at the camp, it was deserted, except for a bedroll that was believed to be that of Arthur Jackson.

Thinking that Jackson was in the bed, Thomas Manning opened fire on the bedroll, thinking that he had killed Jackson. At that time, the Maple Swamp Gang opened fire on the guard. Colonel Thomas Manning, twenty-nine, was killed instantly. Reverend Joel Allen was severely wounded, as were Jesse Bethea, James Finnegan and a man named Johnson who lived at Temperance Hill. As it happened, when the other squads heard the gunfire, they became panic stricken and fled the scene.

When the deserters moved farther into the swamp, some men were sent in to retrieve the dead body of Thomas Manning. It was brought to my attention by the great-great-grandson of Thomas Manning, Houston Manning of Latta that Thomas served in the Civil War during the first part and achieved the rank of major. He was one of seven brothers who participated in the war. Major Manning came home from the war and served with the Home

Guard, where he was promoted to colonel. He was also the father of James Haselden Manning, the first senator of Dillon County.

None of the deserters were killed in this fight; it seemed that this gang was too skilled and ruthless for the local citizens. After that incident, the gang was determined to kill as many of their pursuers as possible.

Captain Charles Fladger was at his home near Dothan Church on January 3, 1865. It was past dark when he decided to walk out to his well for a drink of water. A horseman called from the dark, and when Fladger turned around, he was shot point blank in the chest. As his children ran to their father lying on the ground, covered with blood, Charles Fladger became another victim of the Maple Swamp Gang. Now the Home Guard was without a leader at all; both of their leaders had fallen to this band of deserters. Things looked dismal for the citizens of our homeland.

The next man to suffer the wrath of the Maple Swamp Gang was Dr. Alfred W. Bethea (the great-grandfather of the late A.W. "Red"

Dr. Alfred W. Bethea, killed by the Maple Swamp Gang. *Courtesy of Lesa K. Bethea.*

The Maple Swamp Gang

Bethea). Dr. Bethea was a highly thought of man in the community; he was known to be a good physician, a good farmer and a businessman. Dr. Bethea and Mr. Cade Rogers were traveling by horse and buggy to Little Rock, several miles away. The two were ambushed on the road by some of the deserters, and Dr. Bethea was mortally wounded. Mr. Rogers, who escaped unharmed, drove the horse to Dr. John J. Bethea's home near Little Rock. Dr. John Bethea took charge of the wounded doctor, but he died a few days later on February 18, 1865.

Shortly after this, a party of deserters went to the home of old Malcolm Clark, who was an aged citizen. This was early March 1865. As they called out, Mrs. Clark stepped outside into the dark. She stepped back inside as they fired at the house, barely being missed by the gunfire. Thinking she was dead, the deserters left the premises. The following Sunday, March 12, 1865, the elderly Malcolm Clark was on the road from Marion when he came across a band of the deserters cooking in Samuel Page's lane, near the J.R. Reaves place. (This was near the Buck Swamp Bridge near Floydale.)

As Mr. Clark approached the crew, he recognized the men and pulled out his gun. The leader of the gang said, "Old man, put down that gun and surrender." Clark fired into the bunch, missing his target and killing one of their horses. By this time, they had secured their guns, and several fired at the old man, killing him in the middle of the road. They rode off, leaving him in the road, where he lay for two days. The old men in the community were afraid to touch the old man, thinking that Sherman's bummers and the deserters would kill them also. It was indeed a dark day for what is now Dillon County.

When Dr. John Bethea tried to save the life of Dr. Alfred Bethea, the deserters didn't take too kindly to this. They put out the word that Dr. John would be their next victim. They went calling at his house, and when they could not find him, they ransacked his house and carried off what valuables they could. Up until now, John Bethea had stayed out of the deserter war. He even treated some of their families and just went about his profession. The Maple Swamp Gang didn't know what was in store when they threatened Dr. John Bethea. He was known to be a meek and mild man, but the gang had gone too far. They had aroused a tiger for sure.

We have now seen several members of the Confederate Home Guard killed by the notorious gang, including Captain Charles Fladger, Colonel

Thomas Manning and Dr. Alfred Bethea. Also, a prominent older man named Malcolm Clark had been killed by the gang. Dr. John Bethea and R.K. (Knox) Clark, son of the murdered Malcolm Clark, decided to wage war against the deserters.

They asked for help, and a company of cavalry was sent, and together they succeeded in capturing and killing a good number of the gang. Those who were not captured lay closer to the swamps, and their raids had suddenly ceased. For the first time, the Maple Swamp Gang was under control.

The war was now drawing to a close. Lee's army had surrendered, and the old soldiers began to return home. When the deserters learned that the Confederacy had collapsed, they grew bolder and began to pillage and raid the citizens of the area once again.

When the old soldiers returned home and learned of the things that the gang had done to their families during the war, they vowed that they would not rest until every one of the deserters was killed or hanged for their crimes against their relatives and friends during the time that they were away from home.

The deserters saw that it was not safe for them to remain anywhere in this section, so they stayed away from the towns and villages until the Yankee soldiers began to garrison the towns. They went to the officers at Marion and told them that on account of their Union activities the people of the county were out to kill them and their families.

In the meantime, Dr. John Bethea, Knox Clark and a passing soldier by the name of Lark were diligently searching for members of the gang and were successful at finding some of the deserters. They never told what became of their prisoners, but the prisoners were never seen again. The war was over, but another war had started right here in the place we call our home today. The man called Lark has fascinated me through this research, as very little was ever known about the man and the name is not familiar to this area. During this time, there were some men who came home from the war and became bounty hunters or, in other words, killers for hire. Some I have read about over the years were only called by their last names, if those really were their names. Could it be that Mr. Lark was hired to assassinate many of the Maple Swamp Gang?

The deserters and their families were now terror stricken and continued to appeal to the garrison. The Yankee officers did not know if these people

The Maple Swamp Gang

were murderers or just people who were loyal to the North, so they sent out soldiers to arrest the men who supposedly were persecuting the men who had committed all these crimes against the local citizens. Very few were arrested, and the ones who were arrested were soon released by bribing the Yankee officers.

Arthur Jackson moved to Marlboro County, but Knox Clark was still determined to get him for supposedly killing his father. Clark and some others went to Jackson's house and hid outside the house, waiting for him to come outside. Jackson did come outside, but when he did, he had a child in his arms. The men did not have the heart to shoot the child, so again they waited. The waiting men became tired and fell asleep.

The next morning when they awoke, Jackson was gone, but it was clear due to footprints around where the men slept that Jackson knew they were there and could have killed them in their sleep. It was at this time that Arthur Jackson left the state and moved west.

Knox Clark and Arthur Jackson would meet once more in their lives. Dr. John Bethea moved to Mississippi rather than be harassed by the Yankee officers. After spending several years in Mississippi, John Bethea returned to Mullins, where he lived out his life. John Bethea may have been the man who turned the tide against the Maple Swamp Gang.

Arch Surles did not leave the area but remained in the county and was perhaps one of the luckier men associated with the deserters. He was captured on two occasions, but one time he was given the chance to run for his life. The Home Guard was sure they would shoot him on the run. It was said that Surles began to run, and each time he felt he was going to be shot at, he would fall to the ground. I guess he was pretty smart because it paid off for him and he was able to get away. I had mentioned that a Hugh P. Price was involved with the deserters, but he had little to do with any raids or crimes. Hugh Price became a wealthy man, as did some of the other deserters.

We must remember that this was a time when Americans were fighting against Americans, and a lot of bad feelings wound up right here at home. The war had ended but the problems that had been going on here for some time continued. There had been a lot of hatred built up against the deserters for crimes and murders that had been committed against the local citizens. The deserters now had some protection against the Confederate Home Guard by leading the Yankee officers to believe that they were not criminals but had instead remained loyal to the North during the war.

Arthur Jackson and some of the other members of the gang had moved to a western state to escape the wrath of the Home Guard.

The Home Guard was far from through with some who had caused so many problems for the law-abiding citizens during the war. During the early part of 1865, a company was sent to the Maple Swamp area to arrest Arch Surles, a deserter who had remained nearby. Captain Sandy Ford commanded this squad, and others in this group were Allen Rogers, Theopilus Huggins, J. Mastin Gaddy, Armand LeGette and John Snow. The group arrested Surles at his cabin, and they decided to execute him at once for the crimes of murder, robbery and pillage that the deserters had committed against the community. J. Mastin Gaddy pleaded with the group to spare Arch Surles's life. After much discussion, it was finally agreed to take him to the jail at Marion Courthouse, where he remained until the garrison came. Surles had escaped death twice from the Home Guard.

Some while later, this same squad went to the Hillsboro area (Lake View) and surprised and captured Edward Hill, a Miller and a Grimsley. These three had gone to the house of a man named Barfield, stripped off all his clothes, whipped him unmercifully and burned down his house. They had also committed crimes against others in that community. The squad shot and killed the three; the execution took place between Huggins Bridge and Tabernacle Church by the side of the road.

As time went by, things began to settle down and some of the hard feelings began to go away. Some of the deserters began to show themselves in the communities and villages once again. It took many years for the hatred that had built up during this time to be forgotten, and some took their feelings to the grave.

These men who were known as deserters were looked down on for many years and were never accepted by some who were so loyal to the South and by those whose relatives and friends had been killed by the Maple Swamp Gang. Some of the deserters became wealthy men; some of the local citizens credited their wealth with the things they stole during the war.

The Maple Swamp Gang

Arch Surles gained a large estate after the war and was well thought of among his friends. He was said to become a religious man, faithful to his church, even though some talked harshly about the man and it was said that some desecrated his grave after his death. Archibald Surles died on July 2, 1905. His first obituary stated that he was buried with Masonic honors, but this was later recanted in a future article in the *Dillon Herald* by F.O.S. Curtis of Mackey Lodge 77.

After Reconstruction, Arthur Jackson moved back to Marlboro County and was somewhat involved in politics. It would come to pass that Jackson and Robert Knox Clark, son of the murdered Malcolm Clark, would meet again. It was believed that Jackson had killed the elderly Malcolm Clark. Jackson, while living in Marlboro County, became a client of John Monroe Johnson, a prominent attorney. There was a trial to be held in Marion in which Jackson would have to testify. The clerk of court was none other than Knox Clark.

The day of the trial came, and when Clark administered the oath, he looked Jackson straight in the eye, but Jackson dropped his head and refused to look at Clark. This was the last time the two would ever meet. Robert Knox Clark died in 1888 and is buried at St. Pauls Cemetery at Little Rock. Arthur Jackson died on September 2, 1906, at the age of seventy-two and is buried in Robeson County, North Carolina.

Most everything that has been told and written about the Maple Swamp Gang was told by the "good" citizens of what is now Dillon County. I was not there, so I don't know all the circumstances involving this situation.

Before we close this story, I want to point out a couple of things. In the beginning of the Civil War, there was a young James Jackson, age eighteen, who had married an older woman with children. He had no interest in going off to war. He was confronted with the fact that he would have to join the army, but he refused. James Jackson was found sometime later in a cut-down cornfield with both legs cut off. He bled to death. Another thing that seemed hypocritical to the deserters was that many of the "good citizens" had served little or no time in the military.

The leaders of the Maple Swamp Gang, Arthur and John Jackson's father, was old James Jackson, who also had a brother named John. The "good citizens" paid a visit to old James Jackson, whose brother

Headstone of Robert Knox Clark. *Photo by Helen Lane Wiggins.*

John happened to be at his residence at the time. These men were over sixty years of age.

The citizens demanded to know where Arthur and John were hiding; the old men said they had no knowledge of their whereabouts. After questioning the men for some time with no results, the citizens tied the two old men to their horses and dragged them around until they were dead. It was said their bodies were dumped in a well somewhere in Marion County.

It should also be noted that Arch Surles was listed as a private in Company 1, Regiment South Carolina Volunteers. One source said he was honorably discharged in 1864 due to a serious lung condition. This I have not been able to confirm.

This writer has no opinion on the guilt or innocence of the Maple Swamp Gang. It was indeed a dark period in what would become my

The Maple Swamp Gang

Arthur James Jackson, leader of the Maple Swamp Gang. *Courtesy of Jack and David Jackson.*

home of Dillon County. As in every situation, there are always two sides to a story. As I mentioned earlier, this was another day and time under some very difficult circumstances.

When I wrote this series of articles in the *Dillon Herald*, it created a lot of attention from folks who were related to some of the men who took part on both sides of the fighting. I was asked to speak to several organizations about the Maple Swamp Gang. I spoke to the Pee Dee Genealogy Society in Marion, and to my surprise, twice as many descendants from members of the Maple Swamp Gang showed up for the meeting. Some of them had done considerable research on their ancestors. They did not seem to be ashamed of their ancestors, but many believed they had no part in the war because they were not landowners or kept slaves. Over 600,000 men lost their lives during the Civil War. Was it really necessary?

The Life and Times of David D. Bethea

The name Bethea is one that is very well known in Dillon County. I wouldn't know just what name is the most common in the county, but I would dare say that there are as many Betheas as any other name. I looked in the phone book and there are more people of that name who have phones listed than any other name, and that would not count the members of those households and people who use cell phones or that are unlisted.

There are a vast number of Betheas of both white and black races who live in this area. People who are not familiar with the Bethea name, like people who live in the North, usually pronounce the name differently than people in this area. They pronounce the name more like it is spelled, but in this area, it is pronounced "Bethe." The name Bethea goes back a long way in the history of this county. Two of the earlier Betheas were "Buck Swamp" John Bethea and "Sweat Swamp" John Bethea. This goes back to the 1700s; both men became prominent landowners, and many Bethea descendants came off these two men.

Until about two years ago, I had never heard of the man this story will be about. I had a conversation with David D. Bethea's granddaughter, Dorothy Bethea, and she began to tell me about where he lived a great portion of his life, and to my amazement it was the same farm where I was born and reared. She showed me a book that was written by her nephew, Anthony Cochran, who lives in New York. The book is titled

Kinship Ties and is a very concise account of the African American history of both the Bethea and McRae families who came from and many still live in Dillon County.

Mrs. Bethea let me read her book, and I found it to be very fascinating as I read about people whom I have known and even written, about such as Mr. Robert McRae, on whom I wrote a chapter in my book, *Remembering Dillon County*, titled "The Last Taxi Driver." I talked with Mr. Cochran twice by phone and congratulated him on putting together such a history of these two families, who also include many more names that I could not begin to cover in a chapter. He was quick to say that he had a lot of help in putting this book together, all of whom are mentioned in the book.

In July 2008, I had an opportunity to meet Mr. Cochran at the huge Bethea-McRae reunion held here in Dillon. We had some very good conversations about this unique family. In this story, I will be talking about several David Betheas, so as I speak of this man, I will call him David D. Bethea, which of course was his real name. As I write this article, I bring no reproach upon landowners or people whom I might refer to as "masters."

David D. Bethea was born in the year 1850, one of ten children born to Andrew and Betsy Bethea, both of whom were born in the 1820s. They raised seven of the ten children born to them. David D. Bethea was born a slave, just like his mother and father. They were the property of William Walker Bethea, who was a large landowner who came from one of the original John Betheas I mentioned. In the same year that David D. was born, their owner moved to Clarke County, Mississippi, because the cotton crops were better there. They lived in Clarke County eight years and then moved to Rankin County, where they lived for four years. The Civil War began while they were there.

In 1863, because of the coming of the Northern army, W.W. Bethea moved back to South Carolina to live on the old homeplace, which was now owned by his brother, David Walker Bethea. They traveled to and from Mississippi on wagons pulled by mules. It took weeks for them to make such a trip. In the volume of books called *Kinfolks* published by William C. Harllee in 1937, David D. was referred to as "Uncle Dave," which was a phrase of respect used for African Americans in that time. There is a picture of David Bethea in that book. Harllee said that "Uncle

The Life and Times of David D. Bethea

David D. Bethea, seen here at age eighty-three, was born a slave in 1850. *Courtesy of Anthony Cochran*.

Dave" was eighty-three years old when the picture was taken. He referred to him as a venerable, staunch and Godly black man who belonged to William Walker Bethea and now lives on his master's old home plantation, which was then the home of David William Bethea. David D. Bethea said in his own words, according to Harllee and recorded in *Kinfolks*, that his old master, William W. Bethea, remained on the plantation until "Freedom" and then moved back to Mississippi, where he died several years later.

The Bethea plantation home where William W. Bethea and David W. Bethea lived. *Courtesy of Betty Bethea Day.*

David D. Bethea said, "My father and all his family remained here. I have lived a good part of all the years since 'Freedom' on this place where I was born and am now living." David D. Bethea was a Bethea because his forefathers were given the name Bethea by their masters.

As I researched this story, I came to the realization that this plantation I speak of in this article is the same place I was born on October 8, 1940, and lived until I left home in 1957. Never did it dawn on me that slaves had lived perhaps in the same houses that stood on the farm at that time.

There were some fifteen African American families living on the farm during the time I was growing up, but I never heard the word "slavery" mentioned. It was not talked about, and not until just a few weeks ago when it was brought to my attention did I even think about it. In this story, I will try to tell you a lot more about the life and times of David D. Bethea, a man who was born a slave but had a fine reputation among both black and white. I think you will find it informative about folks who lived in another day and time.

David D. Bethea was a man who never achieved greatness in his life as we might think of greatness today. So many things we take for granted in our lives today, David Bethea never experienced in his time.

The Life and Times of David D. Bethea

He didn't know what it was to walk to the kitchen faucet and get a drink of water or reach into the refrigerator and get a cold glass of tea or lemonade. He lived in poverty his entire life because he was born a slave in the year 1850.

In the last couple of weeks I have talked to some people who actually knew David Bethea, and as I listened to them tell of this man and the memories they had of him in their childhood and early life, I am convinced that he was a good and God-fearing man. As I have already mentioned, he was the son of Andrew and Betsy Bethea, who were the property of William Walker Bethea. I feel that I must point out from my research that W.W. Bethea treated his slaves in a decent manner, and nowhere do I find that they were mistreated.

I don't by any means condone slavery, but we are talking about a different day and time and also a time in history that can't be changed or altered. The purpose of this story is to show how people survived in the only life they knew. William C. Harllee in his *Kinfolks* had much

William W. Bethea, owner of David D. Bethea during slavery. *Author's collection.*

to say about the Bethea genealogy. The Betheas had a great part in settling and developing this land that we call Dillon County today. David D. Bethea is the only African American Bethea mentioned in Harllee's books. David Bethea became a free person at about the age of fifteen when slavery was abolished.

Just because slavery went away, things did not change that much for the former slaves. The only thing they knew was farm work, and farming was so labor intensive that the landowners had to have workers. The slaves became farm workers or sharecroppers. Their homes became sharecropper's shacks provided by the owners. They were paid a small wage or provided a certain amount of acres to work, and any profits left at the end of the season would be divided between the sharecropper and the owner. It was still a hard way of life for an impoverished people.

David D. Bethea and Mary Jane McNeil were married on December 19, 1868, at Little Rock, South Carolina; Reverend J.C. Cousar performed the ceremony. The couple had thirteen children. The first child, Sarah Ann, was born November 12, 1869, and the last child, Josephine, was born July 24, 1894. From this marriage came many generations of African American Betheas and so many other names common to this area today, such as Manning, Alford, Monroe, McRae and many more than I would be able to list.

I spent some time with Mrs. Luvenia Smith Page at her home inquiring about David Bethea. Mrs. Page was born in 1919; she just celebrated her ninetieth birthday. Luvenia and her husband, Randolph Page Jr., lived on this same plantation until her husband's death in 1976. She remembered David Bethea well.

She said he was called "Old Paw" and "Leader Dave" by people on the plantation. She talked about what a good man he was and how he was so well liked by everybody in the neighborhood. She told me where the house he lived in was located on the farm. Her father-in-law, Randolph Page Sr., was his closest neighbor.

I also talked with Mamie Brown Manning, who is eighty-six years of age. Mamie B. Manning married J.C. Manning, who was a grandson of David Bethea. They lived on the plantation for years as well. Mamie was a young girl when she knew David Bethea. I showed her a picture of the man, and she said, "My goodness, that's Old Paw." She remarked about him cutting wood for the widows on the farm to last them through the winter. This was how many folks cooked and heated their homes in that day.

I mentioned that I was also born on this farm in 1940. My father was a blacksmith/mechanic or kind of a jack-of-all-trades. He kept up the equipment on the farm. We really didn't have it much better than our sharecropper neighbors, but we survived also.

David Bethea was still alive when I was born, but he passed away when I was only a year old, so I never knew about him. I remember black folks working in the fields. When I was old enough, I worked right beside them. They were a happy people; they would laugh and joke with one another, and at times they would sing songs of spiritual faith. I really never thought about it like Anthony Cochran mentioned in a conversation, "This was their way of bonding together."

David D. Bethea was said to be an honorable man who treated everyone with respect. I will tell you about his faith in God and his dedication to his church. I have a lot of people ask, "Just where do you come up with these stories?" As I say in my book, *Remembering Dillon County*, "There are a lot of good stories right here in Dillon County that have never been told." David D. Bethea is just one of those stories. This has been quite an amazing story to me as I have studied and listened to people who are old enough to remember this man. David Bethea was born in the year 1850 on land owned by the white Bethea family that has been in that family since perhaps the 1700s. Ninety years later, I was born on that same plantation perhaps a half mile from where he was born. There were two differences in our lives: he was born black and a slave, and I was born white and free. We were both born into poverty.

David Bethea became a free person while still in his teenage years, but he remained right there on the land where he was born. In William C. Harllee's *Kinfolks*, "Uncle Dave" had nothing negative to say about his former masters and later his employers. "Leader Dave," as many of his race called him, married Mary Jane McNeil, and together they had thirteen children on that farm. Eleven were raised to adulthood. His wife passed away in 1928. On February 15, 1941, David D. Bethea passed away at the age of ninety-one.

As I have thought about this man and the many years he spent on this earth, there is more that I would like to have known about him. I doubt that he ever owned a car or even drove one. I doubt that he ever talked on a telephone, and he never experienced the luxury of electricity, because we didn't have electricity on the farm until 1947. But David Bethea was a survivor. Many generations of descendants have come from this man, and from my findings most have been successful, hardworking people. From his family have come teachers, nurses, military people, government workers and many more skilled occupations.

David Bethea was a religious man who attended Bowling Green Church, which is really a story in itself. Bowling Green United Methodist Church, as it is now called, was established in 1855, before the Civil War. The church was started as just a brush arbor on the same plantation that we speak of. Captain David Walker Bethea donated the land and timber where the first church was built sometime before the war. I think this also speaks well of the white Betheas. They wanted their workers to have a place to worship. Andrew Bethea was a minister and was one of the first pastors. Andrew was the father of David Bethea. In Harllee's *Kinfolks*, David D. Bethea said at the age of eighty-three, "I have been an officer of the Methodist Church for fifty-nine years; I have been trying to serve the Lord for sixty-four years. I am trusting in him for my salvation."

I remember well the old church that was located less than a mile down the little dirt road by the house where I lived as a boy. It was back in the woods across a little branch that had a wooden bridge to cross before getting to the church. I remember on Sunday, all the African Americans on the place, as well as some from neighboring farms, would head down the dirt road dressed in their Sunday best. There were just a few cars that might pass, but not very many.

When I was about ten or eleven, the church must have had a revival going on, because I noticed a lot of people passing by on the way to the church. After about thirty minutes, I decided to walk down the road to see what was going on. As I neared the church, I could hear the singing and the music. I just stood in the churchyard for a while. It sure sounded like they were having a great time. I really wanted to go inside, and I would have been welcome, but that was a different time and some things were just not done.

By 1975, most of the people had moved from the farm, and the land was being rented. One by one, all the old houses were torn down. I will

The Life and Times of David D. Bethea

never forget the day I rode out to the farm and the house I lived in was gone. The congregation of Bowling Green Church built a new building out on the paved road, now known as Higgins Road. My wife and I attended a service at the church about five years ago, and so many of the people remembered me. It was so good to see some folks I knew when I was growing up.

To my knowledge, Bowling Green Church is the oldest surviving African American church in Marion or Dillon County. David D. Bethea spent a lot of time helping to construct the old building that these folks spent many joyful times in. The first church burned, but sometime after 1887, another church was erected. I think that David Bethea's faith was what helped him to survive during some very trying times. When I think back to the times when I lived on the farm, I don't remember anybody stealing anything, I don't remember people shooting each

Samuel "Sam" and Helen C. Bethea. Sam was responsible for compiling much of the African American Bethea and McRae family history. *Courtesy of Sam Bethea family.*

other and I don't remember even locking the doors at night. These were hard times, but we didn't know it because so many people lived about the same lifestyle.

There are a lot of people I need to thank for the David D. Bethea story. First of all thank you to Dorothy Bethea, a granddaughter of his who first told me of this man. Dorothy went to college and worked with the Dillon schools for over thirty years. Next, thank you to Anthony Cochran, a great-grandson who lives in New York and wrote *Kinship Ties*, a really good history on the Bethea and McRae families. Also, thank you to people like Luvenia Page, Johnny Page and Mamie Manning, who knew David D. Bethea and shared their memories with me.

The Mill Village

This is a story that began over one hundred years ago. I have written in times past of living on the farm and the hard work that came with such a life. I have told of being very hot in the summer and cold in the winter, I have talked about having very little growing up. We had the essentials in life, such as food and clothing; we went to the doctor only when it was absolutely necessary. This was before the days of Medicare and Medicaid, and we had never heard of health insurance.

I made a statement a while back that when I was a small boy, I thought everybody who lived in town was rich. Of course, there were wealthy people then as well as now, but there were also poor people who lived in town, and a great majority of the poor lived in the mill villages. When I speak of mill villages, I refer to cotton mill villages. In the late 1800s and around the turn of the century, cotton mills began to spring up all over the South.

At the turn of the century, several local entrepreneurs became interested in manufacturing textiles from the cotton produced abundantly in the area. On January 15, 1900, under the leadership of T.B. Stackhouse, the Dillon Cotton Mills were incorporated with a capital investment of $150,000. There were seven local men who also owned stock in the mill. The stockholders were encouraged by the initial success of the mill, so on March 7, 1903, the Maple Cotton Mills was incorporated.

Stackhouse was elected president of both mills, a position he held for three years. He was succeeded by William McCall Hamer. The investment in the Maple Mills was $100,000. That was quite a sum of money at that time. There were nine stockholders in the Maple Cotton Mills. G.D. Barlow was the superintendent of the mills. Under the leadership of Robert P. Hamer, the Hamer Cotton Mill was incorporated on June 10, 1903, with a capital investment of $100,000. Shareholders were W.M. Hamer, R.P. Hamer Jr., D.M. Carmichael and Allen Edens.

William McCall Hamer managed all three companies until November 3, 1910, when a change of executives was announced in the press. W.T. Bethea was elected president of the Dillon and Hamer Mills. W.M. Hamer would retain his holdings in the three mills. Early in 1911, Hamer announced his retirement from further active participation in the cotton mills, and on May 27, the Maple, Dillon and Hamer Mills all became one company called the Dillon Mills. This was one year after Dillon became a county. The sum of $500,000 was involved in effecting the change. The capital stock of the new company was $750,000 and was raised to $1 million in 1922. The total value of the plants and equipment at that time was $1,218,751. The three plants employed three hundred workmen to run their 40,584 spindles.

After the central company was formed, each plant continued to be known by its original name even after 1924, when the Carolina Textile Corporation purchased the complete company and designated each plant by number instead of by name.

Dillon had what was known as the Old Mill and the Maple Mill; both of these buildings are now gone. The term "mill village" came from the fact that the mill owners would build houses for the workers to live in and rent for a fee. These houses were all built identical, with very little yard so they could fit as many houses as possible on the mill land.

All the mill houses except one are gone from the Hamer Mill. Some were demolished, and some were sold to be moved to other locations to live in or for rental property. A lot of houses you see in the area of Arnette Motors, Second Baptist Church and J&J Repair Service were once mill village houses. Some of the people who live in these houses may have worked in one of the mills at one time or may be a relative of someone who worked there. A lot of them have a different look, as they have been added on to and painted a different color. When the houses belonged to the mill, they were either unpainted or painted white. At the beginning, none had indoor plumbing or bathrooms.

The Mill Village

A cotton mill was where cotton was processed into yarn or cloth. The work was hard and unbearably hot, the hours were long and there was no minimum wage. Just like on the farm, these folks had no choice. There was no child labor law in the early 1900s—that did not come into effect until about 1938—so it was not unusual to see children as young as eight years old working in the mill. The families needed the money, because usually the families were large. It was not required to go to school back then, so many children wound up with little or no education. This benefited the owners, because they could work the children for just a few cents a day. Cotton mill workers were referred to as "factory bats" or "lint heads." They were looked down on by the more affluent society. I guess you would say they lived on the wrong side of the tracks.

Very few people made it out of the mill; usually if the father and mother worked in the mill, the children worked in the mill. Most had a small garden spot where they could grow a few vegetables. In this story, we will talk more about the time of cotton mills in Dillon County and

In the early days of the cotton mills, there was not a child labor law. In 1908, at the age of twelve, Etta Squires had been in the mill for three years. *Author's collection.*

A typical mill village family shortly after the turn of the century. Everyone worked but the very young and very old. *Author's collection.*

the people who worked there and the villages they lived in, which a lot of people referred to as the "Mill Hill."

Due to the amount of cotton grown in this area, cotton mills began to spring up in many towns throughout the South. There was a mill in Marion that didn't last as long as the Dillon Mills. There was a mill in Lumberton, North Carolina, and perhaps one of the best-known towns for cotton mills in our area was McColl, over in Marlboro County. McColl was a bustling little town with three cotton mills named the Plymouth Mills.

Back in the fifties and sixties, I had some relatives who worked in the mills at McColl for many years. They too lived in the mill villages there. I remember as a teenager visiting them in McColl, and all the stores on Main Street were filled. Now when you ride through McColl, most of the buildings are boarded up, because the cotton mills are gone and the little town has no industry.

I knew when I started this story that I would have to have some help because I knew very little about the mill village in Dillon. I contacted a couple of fellows whom I have known for a long time who both lived in

The Mill Village

The author with Lonnie Turner and Van Benson. *Photo by Helen Lane Wiggins.*

the mill village growing up and solicited their help in writing this story. Those two men are Lonnie Turner and Van Benson. My wife and I got together with these two men, and we took a tour of what was once the mill village.

I was simply amazed at the way they each remembered where the different families lived; they could call them by name as well as naming their children. Keep in mind that we are talking over fifty years ago. We turned left at Arnette Motors going south, and Lonnie said, "We are now on Main Street of the Mill Hill." This is called Palmetto Street. He pointed out where the house that he lived in once stood. Some of the houses are in really bad shape, having been empty for a long time. Yet some of the folks who have decided to keep these as their homes have kept their homes in pretty good repair. What would concern me is the fact that some of these empty homes might have been taken over by drug addicts.

They pointed out where people would have small stores back in that time. Very few people in the village owned cars, and most walked where they went, so the small stores close by were convenient. We saw where

In 1908, John Roberts had been working in the mill for two years. *Author's collection.*

a man named Frank Causey ran a store for many years on Highway 301, just a quarter of a mile from the Second Baptist Church. The Second Baptist Church was started about the same time that the mills began. I guess you would have called it a mill village church at the time. I remember attending that church for a while when I was a boy of about eight or nine. They had a pastor named Johnny Hooks, who also worked in the cotton mill. I don't guess the church was able to pay him a living salary at the time. Today, the church is a beautiful brick structure with a paved parking lot and good attendance, from what I understand.

Across the railroad as you head toward Main Street was Mr. Ernest Quick's Grocery. That building is still standing but hasn't been used in years. Mr. Quick carried a pretty good line of merchandise, and the customers from the mill village kept him going. Lonnie remembered delivering groceries on his bicycle for Mr. Quick. Also in the store was a post office called Carolina Mills Rural Station. This was where most of the mill people got their mail.

They both pointed out that where Arnette Motors stands and the lot across the street was all mill houses. Both men remembered when the rent

The Mill Village

on the mill houses was five dollars per month. Some of the houses were larger than others and were rented according to the size of the families. We saw where the Old Mill once stood, located between Crown Street and McArthur Avenue. In front of the mill was Palmetto Street. The Maple Mill was located perhaps a mile farther down McArthur Street. Both mills were right beside the railroad; I guess this was for moving the cotton and finished product in and out. Both Lonnie and Van didn't think they had it too bad living in the mill village because all their neighbors lived about the same as they did.

Lonnie's father was Bill Turner; Lonnie said his father went to work in the mill when he was nine years old. He never owned an automobile and walked back and forth to work or rode a bicycle, as did a lot of people who lived in the village. Lonnie said that his father made about twenty-five cents per hour and would work a lot of overtime to support his family. Bill Turner passed away at the age of seventy-two; he worked in the cotton mill some sixty years. Van's father, Van Sr., put fifty-two years in the cotton mill. You might say that these folks had it pretty bad, but folks, they had a job, and this was the only way of life they knew. There was no retirement plan, no 401K and no paid insurance. All they had was that paycheck at the end of the week.

They took the cards that life dealt them and they made the best of it. They were very few who made it out of the mill, but they worked for a better life for their children, and many men and women who were born and reared in the mill village have done very well in life. Since beginning this story, I have heard from a lot of people about this article, and I appreciate your comments and the information you have shared about your life or someone you were related to who worked or lived in the mill village. One fellow shared a story with me, and he said that when you crossed Main Street coming from the village, it was like stepping into another world. He said he went to East Elementary School, and the people from the Mill Hill were treated like second-class citizens. He said he got beat up when he was only in the first grade. He ran away from school and hid under his house. The next day, his father took him to West Elementary School, and that is where he finished his elementary education before moving on to high school. You say you don't know where West Elementary School is? Well, that is what our president calls the "Corridor of Shame." A lot of good people have been through that school and done well in life.

I visited with Mrs. Mattie Lee Turner Garrett, who is now eighty-three. She is the wife of J.C. "Snow" Garrett. She said her family moved from Marion when she was fourteen looking for work. She went to work at the Maple Mill at the age of fourteen running spinning machines. When she was sixteen and World War II had started, she joined the Eighty-second Airborne and packed parachutes during the war. Mattie was voted the "Prettiest Girl" in her division in 1945; this was published in the *Dillon Herald*. Mattie remains a pretty girl.

When she came home, she went right back to the mill and worked there until it closed sometime in the sixties. She couldn't remember exactly when it closed, but when she left all she had was her last paycheck. Mrs. Garrett shared some things with us that I remembered from my time growing up on the farm. She said, "The people in the mill village were like a big family; when a neighbor was sick or down and out, the neighbors were there to help in any way they could."

She said that she had lived in the mill village since she was fourteen; she had not moved more than a mile since that time. The home she lives in is a former mill house but has been remodeled and well cared for. Mrs. Garrett said that a lot of people in the mill village were religious and that they depended on God to sustain them in their daily lives. She said she taught Sunday school at Second Baptist Church for twenty-three years. Later she moved to the Dillon Church of God, which is right down the road from the mill village, and there she has taught Sunday school for thirty-seven years.

I received a call from a Mrs. Mamie James who lived in the mill village. She is eighty-one, and she worked in the mill for a while and also lived in the village. She just couldn't believe that someone was actually writing about the people who lived in the village. She said a lot of people just wanted to forget about the times they lived there, but we both agreed that this is a part of Dillon County history and history can't be changed. Mrs. James said she worked at the post office in Mr. Quick's store for a while. Agnes Norris also worked at the Carolina Mills Rural Station Post Office.

Jean Hayes, who is seventy-two, called to say that when she read the first article, she just sat down and cried. It brought back so many

The Mill Village

memories for her because her parents both worked in the mill and that is where she came up. She is saving the articles to mail to her sisters who also lived in the village and now live out of town.

I mentioned that there were a few people who made it out of the cotton mills seeking a better life. One prime example of this was Mr. Graham Lockamy, who worked in the mill and also did odd jobs on the side, such as collecting and delivering laundry for a dry cleaner that was located in Dillon at that time. After leaving the mill, he tried running a store and maybe a couple of other things, but he wasn't making much progress. Then one day he bought a small junkyard from a man named Albert Brewer. Doesn't seem like a very lucrative profession, does it? Well, that seemed to be the niche in life that Graham Lockamy was searching for, and in a few years that little junkyard became Lockamy's Scrap Metal. For you who knew Graham Lockamy and the Lockamy family, that has become a very successful business over the years.

I need to remind those who perhaps don't know that Graham Lockamy was a devout Christian, and perhaps that is what led to his success. Years later, after the two mills in Dillon closed, Graham Lockamy bought both of the mills. I have never inquired just why he bought the mills; maybe it was for sentimental reasons. The Old Mill was sold to the railroad, and the Lockamy family still owns the property of the Maple Mill. The Old Mill was torn down, and the Maple Mill burned in perhaps one of Dillon's most severe fires some years ago.

When the cotton mills came to Dillon and Hamer in 1900 to 1904, a new way of life began for many people. Most of the people who went to work in the mills came off the farms of what would become Dillon County in 1910. Most were poor sharecroppers who lived a life of hard work from the time they were born. Maybe the change to millwork held some advantage for these folks; they probably made a little more money, and maybe their homes were a little better, but it was still a hard life.

I would imagine that most of these folks had little or no education, but mill life was a steady job. Even as hard as the work was, it was a means of making a meager living to feed their families. I have talked with a lot of people who either worked in the mills or grew up in the mill village. Many have shared their lives in the mill village with me, and even though I grew up as a country boy, I can relate to the things they talked about.

Dillon Cotton Mill employees about 1930. *Courtesy of Bill Lee and Mary King Adams.*

When we look around now and see the things that children have to entertain themselves with, such as video games, go-karts, their own computers, four wheelers and about anything you can think of, we think of the days when we played with whatever was available and most of the time, it didn't cost anything. Everybody's friend, Howard Edwards, came up in the mill village. He talked about Sue Singleton, who had a store where the parking lot of Second Baptist Church is now located. Howard said that Sue was a good-hearted woman and helped a lot of people. I had an opportunity to meet Sue's son Doug at the Dillon Mill reunion. Doug has lived in New Hampshire since joining the military right out of high school. Sue also raised her nephew J.C. Bryant. Howard also talked about a man named Boyd Huggins who operated a store just across the railroad track behind Sue's store. Howard was born in a house beside Huggins's store. He said he remembered when his family got a post office box at the Carolina Rural Station; he said that was a big event in their life.

I talked to Aubrey Small about his time at the mills; Aubrey started work at the Old Mill in 1945 at the age of sixteen. He said that in the summertime,

The Mill Village

Reunion of former mill employees and families. *Photo by Helen Lane Wiggins.*

he would start work at 3:00 p.m. and by 4:00 p.m., his clothes were soaking wet from the heat that the machines gave off and with no air conditioning. He said it was not too bad in the wintertime. The Old Mill closed for a while, and he went to work at the Hamer Mill, where he worked in 1947 and 1948. He then went to the Maple Mill and worked until 1954, when Dixiana Mills came to town, and that is where he spent the next forty years.

A lot of people play golf now for sport and relaxation; people in the mill village played baseball and pitched horseshoes. The Dillon mill village had a pretty good baseball team called the Mud Hens. We will talk more about that team and the players a little later on. A lot of people pitched horseshoes beside Ernest Quick's store. Eddie Howell, who now lives in Folly Beach, was raised in the mill village and worked at the Maple Mill in 1945–46. His family before him also worked in the mill. Eddie said there were ninety-seven houses in the Maple Village when he was there. He started work at the mill for forty cents an hour as a twister-doffer. He said that when he left he was making forty-seven cents an hour.

Dr. Michael Brown shared an interesting story with me about his grandfather, Earl Brown. When Cannon Mills bought the Dillon and

Hamer Mills in 1924, Mr. Earl Brown came to Dillon from Concord, North Carolina, as superintendent of the three mills. Aubrey Small said that Mr. Brown was still superintendent when he started work in 1945. About 1946, Mr. Bill Hyman and Mr. Brown opened WDSC, an AM radio station that operated for many years. I guess because he was the head man, Mr. Brown lived on Cleveland Street. Dr. Brown also told me that Dr. Brian Michaux was the company doctor for the mills. He delivered babies for five dollars each. Prices have changed quite a bit since that time.

Doug Stanton remembers well his days in the mill village. He said that his father, Daniel Stanton, started at the mill as a floor sweeper and went all the way to plant superintendent. Doug talked about a little side business his father had selling soft drinks in the mill. Doug said as a young boy, he pulled the "dope wagon," as folks called soft drinks back then. This was before the days of vending machines. What it amounted to was a wagon with a block of ice on each end. The drinks were kept in the middle to keep them cold. This was also before the days of crushed ice. The Dillon Ice Plant was located just a couple of blocks from the Old Mill.

Doug said he worked in the mill for about three months after high school before he was hired by the Dixie Home store (which later became Winn-Dixie). He became a meat cutter and worked long enough to retire with the company. From there he went to Carl's Food Store, now Carl's IGA. Doug Stanton has been a meat manager for over fifty years and still works full time. Sometime before 1961, the demand for all-cotton yarn and cloth began to fall, and the two Dillon mills began to spin and weave goat hair. The mills became known as the "Goat Mill."

The mills continued to operate until about 1969 before closing their doors for the last time. Now, we will talk about the Hamer Mill, which is the only mill of the three that is still operating. It is Dillon County's oldest industry and has been in operation for 105 years. Hamer Spinning was incorporated in 1903 and started operations in 1904.

Today, the mill still operates with fifty-one employees and runs three shifts. The mill now spins Teflon instead of cotton. Annette Locklear Sanderson and her brother Jerry still work at the mill; both have been there for over thirty years. The mill is now owned by Charles Buie, who once owned five mills, but the Hamer Mill is the only one still in

The Mill Village

The Hamer Spinning Mill bus took employees to and from work. *Courtesy of Margie Mims Griffin.*

operation. The company is now called Charles Craft. Freddie Smith is the plant manager, and Cathy Small works in the office.

The Hamer Mill has a long and rich history in Dillon County. Many people have made a living at the mill for a long time and raised their families through wars, the Great Depression and many recessions we have experienced in this country. My wife and I set out to find some of the old-timers who worked and lived in the Hamer mill village. We visited with Robert and Mary Adams, who now live on Twentieth Avenue in Dillon. Robert, who is referred to as Bob, is eighty-nine years old, and Mary is eighty-three. Bob told us about his days in the Hamer mill village. He remembered when there were fifty-two mill houses in the village. Today, there is only one left; most of the others were torn down or sold and moved to other locations.

Bob said he started work at the mill in 1936; he would have been sixteen at the time. In 1941, when the war started, Bob joined the service and served until the war was over. He said he was lucky; he served all over the European Theater and never got a scratch. He came home and went back to the mill, where he worked in the shipping department and he made twenty-five cents per hour. He met his wife, Mary, and they married in 1946. Mary came from Oxford, North Carolina, with her family to work at Hamer. She worked twelve years until her child was born in 1954. Mary said she worked on production, and in her last days at the mill, she made as much as sixty cents an hour. Both Bob and Mary seem to be in excellent health for their age. Bob said he takes no medicine.

I have talked to a lot of people who said that most of the people who worked in the mills used tobacco of some sort back then. I talked to one lady who said a lot of the women dipped snuff. She said she started to work as just a teenager and was having problems learning to run the machines. This older woman told her that she would never learn until she started dipping snuff. The girl said, "Well, give me a dip." She said she put the snuff in her cheek and about thirty minutes later they were carrying her out. She said she learned the job, but she never dipped anymore snuff.

I talked to a fellow named George Turner whom I have known for quite a few years, and he said he worked at the Hamer Mill for twenty-five years. George said he learned to do about every job there was to do in the mill; he figured the more he knew, the better chance he had of having a job. I remember when I started selling office supplies on the road; Hamer Spinning Mill was one of my first accounts. Mrs. Myrtle Bethea Weatherford and Mrs. Nellie Bracey worked in the office. Both of these ladies are now deceased.

Just about every mill village had a church, and at Hamer, it was the Hamer Church of God. If my years are correct, the church started about 1946. Some forty years later, the church relocated to Highway 301, and it has a good congregation. Before the Church of God was built in the mill village, there was a small chapel that I don't know a lot about or what time it may have started.

My friend Bill Lee wrote a very informative column in the *Herald* about the Hamer Reunion. I also had an opportunity to be at the reunion this year, and later in this chapter, I will share my thoughts about the Hamer Reunion and also a reunion that the Dillon Mills started a few years back. I will also share some more thoughts about the Hamer Mill and the Mim's store that was part of the mill village for a very long time. Some very good people also came off the Hamer Mill Village, and I will be telling you more about these folks.

The Mill Village

Some may be wondering just why I am spending so much time on this story, and I greatly appreciate those who have called and commented about the mill village story. It has been my desire since I began to write articles that the *Dillon Herald* has been so good to publish to recognize people and places that never made the news. The next part of this story will be written by a man who was reared on the Hamer Mill Village. He sent me some information about the village during the time that he was there, and I asked if I could print his memories.

Some months ago, before this story was born, I became acquainted with a man named Dalton Sheppard through the means of a telephone call. He bought several of my books to give to his relatives as gifts. Just a few weeks back at the Hamer Reunion, I had a chance to meet Dalton. I asked him if he would jot down a few memories he had of his time in the Hamer mill village and e-mail them to me. He did just that, and it was a better description than I could ever write, because he lived it. In Dalton Sheppard Jr.'s own words, this is his story of the Hamer mill village:

> *My family lived in the village from about 1939 to 1951. I was 4 years of age when we moved to Hamer from Laurinburg, N.C. It could be said that I spent my most formative years in the village. My memory is that the small village consisted of 50–54 home sites. The sizes, of the homes were 2, 3, and 4 room structures. If each housed an average of 4 people, the population of the village would have been approximately 200 people.*
>
> *There was a small Presbyterian Chapel with a visiting minister on Sunday mornings. Later, a second church, a Church of God was established with a full time minister.*
>
> *There was a small village store, which Mrs. Mims, Margie Griffins mother, owned/managed. The store stocked some food products, personal items, and other essential household items. Residents would travel to Dillon to shop for larger purchases.*
>
> *Many of the residents did not own automobiles in the 40's during World War II. Neighbors, who owned automobiles, would offer transportation to those without automobiles. This usually occurred on Saturdays. I can still remember autos returning from the Dillon shopping trips with the trunk stuffed full of various items, and a large block of*

ice mounted on the rear bumper. Later, the ice company in Dillon would establish a route delivering ice to the community.

Having read about life in other villages, I am amazed that there were so few incidents of violence, theft and other unlawful acts on the Hamer Village during the 40's. There were undoubtedly occasional confrontations, and incidents of over indulgence with alcohol, but we had a constable, Hamp Daniel, who did an excellent job of keeping the peace. The Mill Superintendant, A.J. Wright, was also a strong leader, well respected, and an influential person in the community. He would not tolerate disorderly conduct among the employees/residents of the village.

Charles (Slim) Mims, Margie Griffin's brother, was one of our heroes. He had a country western band, "Slim Mims and his Dream Ranch Boys." They performed at schools, and other venues in the surrounding communities. He was also a disc jockey at WJMX on Florence. But most importantly, using his equipment, he would periodically invite residents, especially young persons in the community, to gather in his mother's back yard to show movies. In inclement weather, they would gather in the village store. He, and his sister Margie, and her husband Floyd Griffin, would occasionally take a group, mostly teenagers, to the Skyline Theater in Maxton, NC, to attend live concerts. We actually would see, in person, movie stars such as the most popular cowboys of that time, Tex Ritter, Lash Larue, and others.

In the mid forties, a resident named Roy Hulon led the effort to establish a Boy Scout Troop, for the village youngsters. Most of the eligible boys eagerly joined. Superintendent Wright, allowed the troop to meet, and store their equipment, in a vacant two room house. Periodically, the troop would take field trips, usually to Moccasins Bluff, on the Little Pee Dee River. On one occasion though, while I was a member, the troop took a special weekend trip to Cheraw State Park.

There was also much focus on sports on mill villages in that era, especially baseball. Hamer seemed to excel. Several baseball players from the village were offered major league contracts. I wish that I could remember all their names, but Curt Allen, Stacy Griffin and Leo (Gabby) Norris come to mind. For many years there was a newspaper article attached to the wall inside the village store, reporting that the

The Mill Village

Hamer Hornets baseball team's won/loss record for that year was like 40 wins, and 4 or 5 losses. I do not recall the exact numbers, but it was impressive.

Most young people living on the village earned their "spending money" working for nearby Farmers, in harvesting their annual crops, mostly tobacco and cotton. The Farmers would come to the village and transport them to the farms, feed them lunch, and return them to the village by sunset. My recollection is that the hourly pay for tobacco harvest was about 25–40 cents per hour, depending on whether you worked in the field, or at the barn. The pay for picking cotton was about 3 cents +/- per pound.

On a personal note: The Sheppard family had been farmers for many years, mostly in North Carolina. My dad Dalton Sheppard Sr. grew up on a farm, and like so many farmers, they lost most of what they owned during the era of the 1930's "great depression." Many of them migrated to the textile villages where they found secure employment and low rent company owned housing.

I remember a large majority of the Hamer village residents, as proud people, with admirable character. There was little that a person would not do for a neighbor in need. My Dad, with his farm background, continued throughout his life to plant large vegetable gardens, as many others did, and share the harvest with their neighbors.

He always had a dream of returning to the farm life that he missed so much. During a period of 15 +/- years, working in the textile mill, he and my Mom saved enough money to make a down payment on a 65 acre farm in the nearby Oakland farming community, while at the same time, supporting a family with five (5) children. Later in life, it occurred to me just what a strong work ethic, and sense of determination, the two of them, as well as many of their village neighbors, really possessed.

Yes, the 1930's, 40's, and early 50's were unusual and difficult times for most people, regardless of where they lived, and especially if you were a parent raising children in such challenging circumstances. But I sincerely believe, that many of the children of those parents, ultimately benefitted from growing up in that environment. I am certain that I did.

Dalton Sheppard Jr. has a long résumé of accomplishments since graduating from Dillon High School in 1954. He graduated from Palmer Business College, served his country in the U.S. Air Force, founded Credit Data Corp. in 1967 and established Sheppard Company, LLC, a commercial real estate firm, in 1989. He was elected to the South Carolina House of Representatives from Lexington County in 1980 and was reelected in 1982. He did not seek election in 1984. Dalton was appointed by President Ronald Regan in 1982 to the Intergovernmental Advisory Council on Education. He also served as chairman of Congressman Floyd Spence's reelection campaign in 1984 and 1986. Not too bad for a boy from the Hamer mill village.

Now we will return to the Dillon mill village and talk about sports in the mill village during the time that the mills were running. Lonnie Turner sent me an e-mail a couple of weeks back about sports during the mill village days, and I don't know of anyone more qualified to talk about sports than him. Lonnie has spent most of his life involved in local sports in this area and could well be the foremost authority on sports in this county. I especially commend him for the years that he has spent working with Little League baseball through his long association with the Kiwanis Club of Dillon. Here, in his own words, are Lonnie's memories of their football-playing days in the village.

> *Being in local sports for so long, I thought you might like to hear more about our football playing field down on the Mill Hill. I mentioned it to you as Van and I rode with you a few weeks ago. Now known as Palmetto Street, Church Street was the most traveled road in the area south of town. I told you and you wrote in the first article that it was the "main street" of the Mill Hill.*
>
> *As you got off 301, a block past the Church of God, ahead of you were two huge Oak trees right smack dab in the middle of the then dirt road. Beyond those trees, the road (we never called it a street) was as wide as Dillon's Main Street, so that became our playing field. The street that runs behind the Church of God now to Palmetto was not there. It stopped directly behind the old church auditorium, which is now the administrative part of the Church complex.*

The Mill Village

Where the road is now, was an empty field between the houses of my sister Pauline (Tom) Johnson and Buddy Moore (father of the late Rev. Jerry Moore). From that point on to the east, there were two houses on the left side of the block...one belonging to Mr. Clarence Carter and the other to Luke and Mamie Taylor. The next section of road is where we played many a ball game after school and on the weekends. We couldn't call it a city block because all we had down there were houses...all the way around a steep curve (where my home was) to the street that leads to South Elementary (not there back then).

Anyway, the road was very wide and our boundaries were the shallow ditches on each side of the road and the west goal was where the street in front of Luke Taylor's house crossed Palmetto. The east goal was just a few feet west of the grocery store that jutted out into the road (run at times by Mrs. Malinda Cook, Teense Rogers, Levi Hyatt, and Lloyd Meekins, just to name a few). There weren't that many cars back then, but when one would come by, we would move to the side and let them pass. Sometimes they would stop and watch. It was a bumpy dirt road most of the time, but every so often the county would send the motor grader down to the mill hill to drag the road. Now talk about a smooth surface, we had it made.

Later when the paving of the streets began, we were all older and both cotton mills were either closed or gone. But, every time I ride down that old street, I am swamped with memories of catching a Charles Norton pass over my shoulder or tackling Jackie Dimery...we didn't have pads, but you know, we never had any injury other than a jammed finger! Memories... wow, and you and your great articles have rekindled them in the minds of most of us who spent many hours playing in the street and staying out of trouble. Thanks again for jogging our memories. Your articles are always bright spots in the Thursday editions of the Dillon Herald!

I want to thank Lonnie for his memories from the mill village days.

I mentioned in the first of the mill village series a baseball team that the Dillon mill village had called the Mud Hens. The mill villages across the South played a lot of baseball because that was about their only means of recreation. Doug Stanton and Van Benson shared their memories from the days of the Dillon Mud Hens. No one seems to know when the team actually got started, but it must have lasted for a long time. The time we are talking about would have been in the forties and early fifties. Mr. George Lewellen was the coach of the team; he passed away in 2004. Some of the pitchers were J.C. Burney, R.B. Hyatt and Lamar Smith. Some of the catchers were Harold Caddel, Jack Simpson and John C. Morris. Johnny Williams was said to be an outstanding player and played first base. J.C. Strickland played second base.

Cecil "Pete" Martin played shortstop, "Speedy" Davis played center field, Earl Quick was in right field and Wally Lewellen played left field. Other men who played for the Mud Hens were Norman "Booty" Jackson, Mac Benton, Howard Caulder, Paul Hyatt, Cotton Allen, Malcolm Huggins, Sim Caulder, Carl Morris and Clyde Coates. Doug Stanton and Tommy Morris played a little for the Mud Hens as just young boys. The batboy was Van Benson. One of the teams that the Mud Hens played was a team from the Carolina area. Other teams were Gapway from the Mullins area and teams from Latta, Little Rock and McColl. As I understand it, Dillon had a town team that played against the Mud Hens. Also, they played a little against the Dillon Border Belt team when the league was operating.

The baseball field was located where the Johnny Hood car shop is located on Highway 301; of course the gas company was not there at the time.

As we wind down the mill village story, I feel privileged to have shared with you a story about another day and time in the history of Dillon County and the lives of some good, hardworking people who survived some hard times to provide for their families. I have heard from a lot of people about this series, some who actually worked in the mills themselves and some whose families worked in the mills to try and make a better life for their children. We have talked about one hundred years of history in this county, and the mill at Hamer still operates as it has for over one hundred years.

The Dillon Mills closed about 1968 or 1969, and both of these mills are no longer there, but they hold a lot of memories for many people. We visited with James and Carol Oates Baker, who still live in the mill village in Dillon. Both of their parents worked in the mill. Carol lived in the Hamer mill village for a long time and worked in the mill herself. James joined the navy and made a career, retiring after twenty-three years of service. James and Carol live in a house once owned by Carol's parents, Charlie and Viola Davis Oates, on Crown Court. Over the years, James has done extensive work to the house, having added a smaller mill house to the back of this house, and has made a nice-looking home. James and Carol will celebrate their fiftieth wedding anniversary on December 5.

I received an e-mail from Pat White, who lives in Cheraw. We got together and had lunch last week, and he shared some good stories about coming up in the mill village. His father was Johnny White, who worked in all three mills at one time or another. Johnny, like a lot of others, started at the bottom and worked his way to supervisor. A lot of people I talked to remembered Johnny and said he was a good man to work for.

Pat said that during his childhood, his family lived in all three mill villages. While in high school, Pat worked at the South of the Border Motel as a Pedro. He worked hard, and the tips were good. He saved his money and went to Clemson College. He went to work with Foxboro Computers at the J.P. Stevens plant in Wallace. When the Stevens plant closed, Pat went on the road and worked for the company several years before retiring in 1999.

About 1957, due to the decline for all-cotton material, the two mills in Dillon started a new venture. They started spinning goat hair. This hair was imported from overseas and was mixed with cotton to make a satin-looking material. The mills soon took on a new name: the Goat Mills. There was much talk about people who worked at the Goat Mills. I still remember the story of the young boy who was passing the mill with his father. He looked at his dad and said, "Dad, do they really make goats there?" Not too long after the mill switched to the goat hair operation, people who worked there began to get sick. Some were hospitalized with what was called the "Goat Fever." It was discovered that the sickness was really anthrax, which was a pretty deadly disease. It came from the imported goat hair; from that point, shots were administered to the employees to control the problem. I don't recall anyone dying from the disease, but it made them pretty sick.

Sarah Cook called to say that she worked at the Goat Mill for about five years and she hoped that I would mention the Goat Mill. Dean Davis came by and talked about her time at the mills and said she also worked there after the change to goat hair.

Boys from the mill village are, *left to right*: Hamer Rich, Carlisle Owens, Billie Freeman, Floyd Baker, Carl Turner and Marion Carter. *Courtesy of Doug Stanton.*

I talked to Earl Dubois, who shared stories about his time at the Goat Mill. Earl said he went to work there about 1961 and worked until the mill closed about 1969. Earl's wife, Mary, also worked at the mill. When the mill closed, both went to Carpostan in Lake View, which was just getting started. They both worked there until Carpostan closed its doors recently. The last year the Dillon Mills operated, they made bags for sand that were used in the Vietnam war. Dan Poole was the superintendent at that time and became one of the founders of Carpostan Industries.

A lot of the workers went to Dixiana Mills and some went to Burlington Industries, but these are also gone now. Textiles, which played such a great part of life in the South, is almost a thing of the past now. These jobs have gone overseas in search of cheaper labor. I hear of jobs in these third world countries paying twenty-five cents an hour, but there was a time when folks worked in the cotton mills of Dillon for the same amount of money.

When we think about the high unemployment figure in Dillon County at this time, it seems staggering. Maybe I don't see the real picture, but I

The Mill Village

am convinced that a certain percentage of these people just don't want to work or are not willing to work at a lower-paying job. There are those who would prefer to live off public assistance or ride the unemployment check as far as they can take it. There was a time when there were no programs such as this, so people worked long and hard in the cotton mills of Dillon County because they didn't have any other choice.

I hope you have enjoyed my story on the mill village; this is perhaps a story that would never have been told about some good people who just came from the "wrong side of the tracks." I hope that this story has been able to uncover some of the *Hidden History of Dillon County*.

About the Author

A little over seven years ago, Carley Wiggins sat down and wrote a simple article that was published in the *Dillon Herald*, a small, biweekly newspaper in the northeastern part of South Carolina. As far as he knew, that would be the one and only thing he would ever write for publication. When the article came out in the paper, the response from readers was overwhelming. Wiggins was encouraged by the paper and readers to write more.

Without a degree of any kind and not one day of journalism experience, Wiggins began to write a weekly column. Most were about little-heard-of places and people in the Pee Dee area. Wiggins began to write stories about people and places in Dillon County that had never been told before. Today the number of articles he has written numbers nearly four hundred, many in series form and some lasting as long as twenty weeks.

Carley Wiggins has won six major awards for his writing and on January 6, 2011, was presented with the award he is most proud of, as he was named Dillon County Citizen of the Year for 2010. He published

About the Author

one book in 2008, entitled *Remembering Dillon County*. For a man who never considered himself a writer, he has heard from readers in over twenty states and several foreign countries. At the age of sixty-two, Carley Wiggins found a new career as a freelance writer and from the encouragement of his readers now offers his second book as a permanent record of seven of his more popular articles for you to enjoy, called *Hidden History of Dillon County*.